KNOWLEDGE AND INFALLIBILITY

KNOWLEDGE AND INFALLIBILITY

J. L. Evans
Professor of Philosophy
University College, Cardiff

ST. MARTIN'S PRESS NEW YORK

Typeset in Great Britain by
Vantage Photosetting Co Ltd
Southampton and London
Printed in Great Britain

Library of Congress Catalog Card Number 78-18468

First published in the United States of America in 1979

Library of Congress Cataloging in Publication Data

Evans, J. L.
  Knowledge and infallibility.

  Bibliography: p.
  Includes index.
    1. Infallibility (Philosophy) 2. Knowledge, Theory of.
I. Title.
BD234.E9   121   78-18468
ISBN 0-312-45906-8

Contents

Acknowledgements

Many friends have helped me at various stages in the writing of this book. At Cardiff, I have benefited greatly from discussions with colleagues in the Department of Philosophy, and especially with Mr Donald Evans who also commented in detail on an earlier draft; Mr W. O. Evans and Mr H. M. Quinn of the Department of English and Professor F. J. Jones of the Department of Italian gave me invaluable advice, particularly on matters of presentation. Outside Cardiff, Professor R. I. Aaron of Aberystwyth and Professor S. Körner of Bristol assisted me with advice and encouragement. To Professor Sir Alfred Ayer of New College, Oxford I owe a threefold debt: for what I have learned from his writings, for prompting me to write this book and for his sustained interest at every stage in its preparation. My son, Mr D. L. Evans, made many suggestions which I was glad to accept.

I would like to thank Dr C. W. L. Bevan, Principal of University College, Cardiff, not only for his constant encouragement, but also for his readiness to arrange relief from my administrative duties while I was writing this book, and Professor T. H. McPherson for undertaking them in my place.

Finally, I acknowledge with gratitude my debt to previous writers, too many to enumerate here, on the topic of knowledge, but particularly to J. L. Austin and Gilbert Ryle.

Cardiff   J. L. Evans
April 1978

Introduction

This book is written both for students of philosophy and for the general reader. It assumes little or no previous knowledge of the subject, yet tries to make intelligible to non-specialists some of the contemporary as well as some of the traditional discussions on the topic of knowledge. As a teacher of philosophy I have found that students are often puzzled by the diversity of views expressed on the concept of knowledge both in the writings of traditional philosophers and in the many books and articles published on the subject in the last twenty years or so. They are further puzzled by the remarkable disparity between the assumptions about knowledge which we make in everyday life and the things which many philosophers say when they theorise about knowledge, and also between the use of the concept by historians and scientists, for example, and the speculations of many philosophers on knowledge. I have tried, therefore, to provide a critical review of some of the main developments specifically with a view to trying to explain why this disparity has arisen. The main reason for its prevalence is, I believe, the acceptance by many philosophers of certain long standing misconceptions or myths which have hindered our understanding of the concept of knowledge. The influence of these myths can be detected in contemporary as well as in traditional philosophy: their continued survival, in whole or in part, is the justification for this attempt to eradicate them.

The primary myth is that knowledge must be infallible in the sense that we can have knowledge only where there is not the possibility of being mistaken, that we can be right only where we cannot be wrong. The second myth is the description of knowing as an experience or as a mental act, something which we do. The conjunction of these two myths results in a severe restriction of the extent of our knowledge and in an equally severe restriction on the ways in which knowledge may be acquired. We can know only what cannot be false, and the only procedures which can yield knowledge are those which are immune from the risk of error. The third myth is that knowledge is a mental state or mental attitude which can be equated with being sure, or at least involves being sure. In contrast with these positions is our widespread practice of allowing that there is, in principle, little or no restriction on the areas where we can get knowledge, and that familiar procedures such as observation and inference, though not exempt from error, can often provide knowledge.

A consequence of the acceptance of some or all of these myths is that the relationship between knowledge and belief is misunderstood. A further consequence is that philosophers frequently seek to replace the concept of knowledge as understood and used in everyday life by a technical, philosophical concept which fits in with their other theories. I do not myself think that it is within the province of philosophy to alter or seek to replace the concepts in common use: its business is, rather, to increase our understanding of these concepts, particularly by exhibiting their relationships with kindred concepts. Nor do I see how the substitution of a technical concept for a familiar one can in any way illuminate it: on the contrary, it can lead only to its distortion. I defend, therefore, the assumptions about knowledge which we commonly make, and try to show that they survive the challenge from the theories based on the myths to which I have referred.

1 Some Problems about Knowledge

The reader who is unacquainted with philosophical speculation about knowledge might well think that a discussion of the nature of knowledge should start by giving a clear indication of what it is, and this expectation might well be expressed by asking for a definition of knowledge. Surely, it might be said, before we can profitably consider and assess rival theories about knowledge, it would be appropriate to begin with a definition which might bring out the essential features of knowledge and enable us to distinguish it from related notions with which it might be confused. There are, however, several reasons why this natural expectation must remain unsatisfied.

The first obvious rejoinder which we could make is that the proper place for a definition of knowledge would be at the end of our inquiry rather than at the start. Explorers, we might point out, do not start their explorations with a worked-out map of the territory which they are intending to explore; on the contrary, the detailed map can be produced only after the exploration has been successfully completed. Those explorers who set out in search of the source of the Nile, for example, could not already have known the source when they set out. But it would be absurd to suggest that they set out in utter ignorance of what they were looking for: they had hunches which they were trying to convert into certainties. So we, embarking on an exploration of the concept of knowledge, are not, at the start of our inquiry, assured of our conclusions, as our ability to offer a definition of knowledge would imply; nevertheless we are not travelling in wholly unfamiliar territory. We are, after all, dealing with a notion which is already broadly familiar in everyday life, and signposts are not wholly lacking to guide us. It is not the case that without a map in the form of a definition we do not and cannot know where we are going.

In the second place, it might be said in reply to the request for a definition that to provide one might well prejudge some of the issues which should be kept open at the start of an inquiry into knowledge. Philosophers have, indeed, frequently attempted to define knowledge in terms of other related notions such as belief; it has been suggested, for example, that knowledge can be defined in terms of 'justified, true belief'. The adoption of such a suggestion would, however, meet with the objection from other philosophers that knowledge is a unique, unanalysable notion, the nature of which would inevitably be distorted by any attempt to define it in terms of any other notion. Further, such an attempted definition could be successful only if the notion of belief was already understood. Indeed, this position that knowledge is *sui generis*, i.e. not analysable in terms of anything else, has been widely held from the start of philosophical speculation about knowledge. Thus the question whether knowledge is equivalent to, or definable in terms of some sort of belief, or to belief qualified in certain ways, is a substantial issue which calls for detailed consideration; it should not be prejudged by providing a definition in advance of such consideration. Similar rejoinders could be made to attempts to define knowledge in terms of notions other than belief.

In the third place, it would not be helpful if we were to try to meet the request for a definition simply by providing an inventory of the sorts of things which we might claim to know, for example that two and two make four, that grass is green, that the Battle of Waterloo was fought in 1815, etc. Should we attempt to provide such a list we would immediately be open to the rejoinder, 'Surely, if you are able even to start compiling a list of the things which we know, you must already know what knowledge is: otherwise how could you decide to include this particular item in the list and to omit another?' In other words, the ability to provide a list of the sorts of things which we know presupposes the possession of some criteria by means of which selection and omission can be done, and, it could be added, the possession of such criteria must constitute at least part of what is meant by 'knowing what knowledge is'. In any case the mere provision of an assortment of items of knowledge would not take us very far: we would very soon run into controversy as to whether a particular item should be included, and we would not for long be able to avoid introducing some criteria or principles to settle the issue.

Further, the fact that such a list would inevitably be an assortment might well in itself raise an immediate difficulty. In the simple list which was given by way of illustration earlier of the sorts of thing which most people would claim to know, there was an example of mathematical knowledge (knowing that two and two make four), an example of historical knowledge (knowing that the Battle of Waterloo was fought in 1815) and an example of something which is known by observation (knowing that grass is green). The question which might well be raised by someone when confronted with such a list is the question whether these are examples of knowledge in the same sense of the term: it might well be contended that there are obvious differences between knowing the truth of mathematical propositions and knowing the truth of historical propositions, for instance. One mathematical proposition is just as good as any other as an example of mathematical knowledge; we can just pick at random since, superficially at least, we do not distinguish between those mathematical propositions which are known or can be known and those which can only be believed to be true. But one historical proposition is not as good as any other as an example of historical knowledge; the distinction between what is known and what is merely believed clearly applies in this context. Thus we might claim to know the dates of Cromwell or Winston Churchill, but we could hardly claim to know the dates of Lycurgus or King Arthur. We might cite our knowledge of the date of the Battle of Mons as an example of historical knowledge but not the date of the Battle of Marathon. It might well be misleading, therefore, to include mathematical and historical propositions indiscriminately in a list of things which we might claim to know. Or again, it might be suggested that there must be some difference between a proposition the truth of which is discovered by observation (e.g. 'grass is green') and a proposition the truth of which seems to be discoverable independently of observation (e.g. 'two and two make four'), so that perhaps it might be the case that the source of our knowledge of a proposition might have considerable bearing on its status. We seem, therefore, already to have sufficient reason to be suspicious of any random list of items of knowledge such as the one offered above. We should at least sort such items into various categories and not simply assume that any one example, such as one based on simple observation like 'grass is green' is exactly on a par with any other example, such as 'two and two make four', or that each category provides us with instances of knowledge in exactly the same sense.

The point which is already emerging is the apparent complexity of the notion of 'knowledge': it does not appear to be a simple notion like 'yellow' or 'desk'. The recognition of this fact enables us to make the further reply to anyone expecting a definition of knowledge at the start of an inquiry into its nature, namely that the very complexity of the notion would render any simple definition unhelpful, if not positively misleading. We must now look more closely at the complexity of the notion of knowledge.

It is typical of any term which arouses philosophical interest that it is used in a wide variety of ways. Examples of this abound. The term 'good' has a bewildering variety of uses: we use it of people ('Jones is a good man'), of things ('that is a good knife'), of qualities ('conscientiousness is a good quality'), etc. Sometimes it is used in a specifically ethical context and sometimes in non-ethical contexts. Or again, the word 'meaning' has a wide range of uses. Sometimes it is used as a rough synonym of 'intends' as in 'he means to call on you tonight', sometimes it approximates to 'implies' as in 'inflation means that books will cost more'; we speak of the meanings of signs, symptoms, words, sentences, etc. It is not, therefore, surprising that clusters of problems of philosophical interest arise concerning the notions of goodness and meaning. The same situation arises in the case of knowledge. In everyday life the verb 'to know' is used in a variety of ways; for example we speak of knowing people (e.g. knowing Churchill), of knowing places (e.g. knowing Blackpool), of knowing truths or facts (e.g. knowing that Great Britain is an island), and there is no obvious reason why we should assume that the verb 'to know' is used in exactly the same sense in these cases, though we would not expect to find that there was nothing in common between them. Or again, the verb is sometimes used to indicate the acquisition of a skill of some kind, as when we say that someone knows how to play Poker, as opposed to its use to refer to the fact that someone has learned some truth, as when we say that someone knows that the atomic weight of gold is 197·2. Here, too, it is not immediately obvious that the verb 'to know' is used in exactly the same way in both instances. It might, therefore, be conceded that any attempted definition which aimed at comprehensiveness could only mislead in that it might mask distinctions which need to be drawn.

It is also typical of any notion which is of philosophical interest, in the sense that it generates philosophical problems, that it should be intimately related to a variety of other concepts. Thus the notion of freedom is closely connected with such concepts as 'choice', 'responsibility', 'obligation', etc. It is of great importance to recognise that it is impossible to get more than a superficial understanding of, say, the notion of freedom if we isolate it from its kinsfolk and attempt to study it on its own. It might, indeed, be contended that a major part of understanding the notion of freedom, as with any notion of philosophical interest, is precisely understanding its relationships with kindred concepts. The same applies to knowledge. It is closely connected with such other notions as intelligence, certainty, conviction, belief, learning, understanding, to name only a few, and equally the attempt to separate it from its fellows with a view to studying it in isolation cannot yield fruitful results. Understanding what knowledge is consists very largely in understanding its relationships with such notions as 'intelligence', 'certainty', 'belief', etc.

It appears, therefore, that the simple question, 'What is knowledge in itself?', whether or not this is a disguised attempt to ask for a definition of knowledge, is unlikely to result in a profitable inquiry. This is so, I have suggested, for the following reasons:

(a) If more is required of a definition of knowledge than an indication of how one proposes to use the term 'knowledge', the only possible place, if at all, for such a definition is at the end of our inquiry rather than at the start.

(b) A simple definition which involves defining knowledge in terms of other concepts such as belief (e.g. 'knowledge is true, justified belief') would prejudge substantial issues.

(c) Such a definition would inevitably fail to do justice to the complexity of the notion of knowledge.

(d) It would misleadingly suggest that the notion of knowledge could profitably be studied in isolation from other concepts with which it is intimately connected.

The alternative method of inquiry, which I propose to adopt, is to look at the range of problems concerning knowledge which have traditionally exercised philosophers, paying particular attention to the reasons why these problems have arisen. These problems may conveniently, if somewhat arbitrarily, be mentioned under the following headings:

1   THE EXTENT OF OUR KNOWLEDGE

A question which we might naturally ask is 'What is the extent of human knowledge?' Are there any necessary restrictions on the possible range of knowledge so that, for example, we can say that we have knowledge of the present and perhaps of the past but not of the future? Are there, as some philosophers have thought, compelling reasons for the conclusion that nothing which is subject to change can ever be known, so that the possibility of acquiring knowledge is confined to what is permanent and unchanging, if there should be any such things? Some philosophers, for instance, have advanced arguments designed to establish the view that knowledge is attainable only in such abstract disciplines as logic and mathematics, while others have resolutely defended our everyday practice of claiming to know the truth of a wide variety of factual propositions, for instance that the Battle of Waterloo was fought in 1815, that the coal bucket is empty, that the desk in the next room is made of teak, etc. To other philosophers, again, knowledge is just an unattainable ideal: we have to be content, so they insist, with belief or probability or opinion. There is, thus, a great deal of divergence, historically, in the answers given to the question of the range of human knowledge, varying from the sceptical position that knowledge is, for a variety of reasons, unattainable, to the more generous view that there is in principle little or no restriction on the range of things which can be known.

2   THE SOURCES OF OUR KNOWLEDGE

Are there many possible sources of knowledge or does it all originate from a single source? One of the persistent philosophical problems concerns the status of sense-perception and its relation to knowledge. Whereas some philosophers have advanced arguments to justify the common-sense claim that perception or observation is a possible, indeed the primary, source of knowledge, others have contended that there is an endemic weakness in perception, namely its proneness to error, which completely debars it from providing knowledge. The fact that judgements based on perception are sometimes mistaken—for example, I might erroneously think that a straight stick immersed in water is bent—is thought by many to disqualify perception as a source of knowledge. Alternatively, we might ask, perhaps with an eye on mathematics and logic, whether the human mind has the power in itself, independently of observation, to acquire knowledge. Some philosophers, as we shall see, have concluded that the mind is endowed with this power, while others, rejecting this claim, have persisted in the view that knowledge, if it is possible at all, must originate only from sensation. Other possible sources of knowledge, whose claims have often been advanced, are memory and imagination, for example.

3 PSYCHOLOGICAL QUESTIONS ABOUT KNOWLEDGE

Is knowing to be thought of as some kind of mental state or disposition or is it, sometimes at least, some sort of mental act or activity which we can perform? Sometimes it has been regarded as comparable, as a mental state, with, say, 'enjoyment'; sometimes as comparable, as a mental activity, with, say, 'finding' or 'discovering'. Although it might appear at first sight that knowing is an activity, something which we do, it is possible that, in thinking this, we have been misled by the grammatical rule that verbs denote some activity into assimilating 'psychological' verbs such as 'to know' or 'to believe' to ordinary transitive verbs such as 'to dig', which clearly denote an activity of some kind. It is significant that, whereas it would be appropriate in answer to the question 'What were you doing this morning?' to reply 'I was digging the garden' or 'I was searching for my missing pen' or 'I was looking at the Test Match', it would be inappropriate to reply 'I was knowing that Madagascar is an island' or 'I was knowing that two and two make four'. If the assimilation of psychological verbs to ordinary transitive verbs is mistaken, it may well be that knowing is never to be described as an activity but should always be regarded as some sort of mental state. Or again, it might well be that the disjunction 'either a mental state or a mental act' does not apply to knowing, which would then have to be categorised in some other way.

If, however, we were to conclude that knowing is a state of mind rather than a mental act, the question will arise as to what are the characteristics of such a state. For example, is 'being sure' or 'being convinced' a necessary condition of knowing, such that we would not allow a claim to knowledge unless it were accompanied by conviction? Or, is 'being sure' merely an accidental accompaniment the absence of which would not disqualify a claim to knowledge, or could it be that the presence or absence of conviction or being sure is simply irrelevant to our understanding of knowledge itself? On the one hand, there is the fact that, whereas we would not regard some measure of doubt or uncertainty as disqualifying a claim to belief, we would reject the conjunction of a claim to know something with the admission that the claimant was uncertain as to the truth of what he claimed to know. Thus, 'I believe so-and-so, though I'm not too sure of it' is acceptable; 'I know that so-and-so is the case, but I'm rather uncertain of it' is not. Such considerations might well lead us into concluding that conviction is a necessary accompaniment of knowledge. On the other hand, it might appear very strange to ask a man who claimed to know something whether he was sure, or how sure he was: such questions, it might be thought, are appropriate to situations where a man says that he believes something but irrelevant to a situation where a man claims knowledge. A further possibility is that the introduction of the notion of 'being sure' as a positive accompaniment of knowledge is due to the mistaken identification of the absence of one thing with the presence of something else. That is, the fact that knowledge, as opposed to belief, is characterised by the absence of doubt does not, in itself, indicate that knowledge must be accompanied by the presence of a positive feeling of 'being sure' or 'being convinced'. We shall also have to consider the feasibility of identifying knowing with being sure or being convinced, as opposed to regarding 'being sure' merely as an accompaniment of knowing. If this move were possible, we would then be able to talk equally of knowing so-and-so and being sure of so-and-so.

Finally, whether we regard knowing as a mental state or as a mental act, we shall have to face the problem of the recognition of knowledge when it occurs. How can we tell when we know something or when someone else knows something? Are we, for example, to say that knowing is something which identifies itself, so that the knower cannot help knowing that he knows? If so, why is it not also true that error, the opposite of knowledge from one point of view, is also self-identifying? How is it that sometimes we think we know and, on reflection or in the face of criticism, have to withdraw the claim to knowledge?

4 RELATIONSHIPS WITH OTHER CONCEPTS

(a) Belief. We often think of knowledge in everyday life in conjunction with other notions such as belief and opinion, and they are frequently grouped together by philosophers and psychologists under the heading of 'cognitive' activities. It might be assumed from the fact that they are sometimes used interchangeably that there is no radical difference between knowing and believing, so that knowing could properly be regarded as a specific variety of believing. On the other hand, although we frequently think of them in conjunction, there are also occasions when we contrast them. Thus a situation might arise when it would be appropriate to say that someone does not know so-and-so but merely believes it. Further, there is the much-noticed fact that, whereas we see no incompatibility in someone saying that he believes so-and-so but of course may be mistaken, we see a flat contradiction in someone saying that he knows something but that of course he may be wrong, or indeed in saying that he knows something and may of course be right. In other words, we allow that what we believe may be true or may be false but insist that what we know can only be true; 'false knowledge' is disallowed. Such considerations as these might lead us to conclude that there is some radical difference between knowledge and belief, a difference of *kind* and not just of *degree*, which prohibits any attempt to define knowledge as any sort of belief.

If, then, we were to conclude that the difference between knowing and believing is a radical difference of kind, this might imply that their 'objects' are also radically different, i.e. that the things which can be believed can never be known, that there is a frontier between the territories of knowing and believing which cannot be crossed. Alternatively, it might suffice to distinguish between the mental states of knowing and believing without introducing a corresponding difference between their objects, in which case it could be possible for the same thing to be known by one person and merely believed by another, for example I might know that Madagascar is an island and you merely believe that it is, or it could be possible for the same thing to be believed by me at one time and known by me at another, for example I might at one time merely believe that Lima is the capital of Peru and, after investigation, come to know that it is. The relationship of knowledge to belief is clearly a complex one which needs discussion.

(b) Certainty. We clearly have to distinguish between saying, on the one hand, 'I am certain that . . .' and 'it is certain that . . .' on the other. The first expression more or less identifies certainty with 'being sure', which we have already mentioned as a psychological accompaniment, so it is often claimed, of knowing. But the second expression should not be taken to refer in any way to someone's attitude to a given proposition. It might be said that it is relevant to the status of the proposition which constitutes what is known rather than to the knowing of it by an individual. There is clearly a difference between saying that someone knows p and saying that p is certain. This can be seen simply by realising that from the fact that we can say that it is certain that so-and-so is true, it does not follow that I or any other individual knows it. From the fact that it is certain that the Battle of Waterloo was fought in 1815, it does not follow that I or any other individual knows it. Yet there is clearly some connection between the notions of certainty and knowledge. What exactly is implied by the notion of certainty? Does it, for example, imply infallibility or incorrigibility, as has often been suggested? In other words, is it a necessary condition of crediting someone with knowledge that there is not the possibility of his being wrong or mistaken? An affirmative answer to this question might involve us in accepting either or both of the following positions: first, it might mean that we must impose severe restrictions on the range of things which can be known. Thus we might have to restrict the possibility of knowledge to those things which from the nature of the case could not be otherwise—to propositions such as '$2+2 = 4$', 'if X is a bachelor, X is unmarried' (so-called 'necessarily true' propositions). This would involve rejecting the possibility of acquiring knowledge of any proposition which is only 'contingently' or 'accidentally' as opposed to 'necessarily' true, indeed any factual proposition such as 'It rained in London yesterday' or 'Harold

was killed at the Battle of Hastings'. Secondly, it might mean that we must restrict knowledge to those ways or procedures of knowing which are such that they guarantee themselves and rule out the possibility or error, if indeed there are such procedures. This would involve rejecting perception, for instance, as a possible means of acquiring knowledge on the grounds that it is subject to error, that judgements based on perception may be false. Conversely, it might be that the distinction between fallible knowledge and infallible knowledge is a mistaken one, and that the introduction of the notions of infallibility and incorrigibility in this context serves only to distort our ordinary sense of knowledge. Perhaps the fact that there is always the possibility of error, that the person who tries to achieve knowledge may fail to do so, does not in any way prevent us describing his success in achieving knowledge, when he does succeed, as knowledge in the most complete sense. The impossibility of failure is not a necessary condition of success.

(c) *Understanding.* Traditionally too much emphasis may have been placed by some philosophers on the use of 'knowledge' when we refer to someone knowing a particular truth or fact, for example that Great Britain is an island, that Paris is the capital of France, that this desk is made of wood, etc. The danger in this tendency is to divorce the notion of knowledge from that of understanding. Certainly, when we speak of historical knowledge, for instance, we do not intend to refer to an assortment of isolated bits of accredited information; we imply that the person credited with historical knowledge is able to some extent to relate these bits of information into some sort of whole or picture. The same is true of scientific knowledge, which can hardly be described as a random collection of isolated bits of information. This suggests that more is involved in knowledge than merely getting something right, for example correctly answering the question 'What is the capital of France?' by saying 'Paris', where the correct answer may have been arrived at by guessing. Getting the answer right is, of course, a necessary condition, but in itself it does not seem to be enough for knowledge. What more, then, is needed?

5   MULTIPLICITY OF USES

We saw earlier that we distinguish between knowledge of truths or facts, for example knowing that Caesar crossed the Rubicon, and knowing people or places or things. We also distinguish between knowing truths and knowing how to do something, for example knowing how to scull. These customary distinctions have given rise to considerable philosophical controversy. The first distinction, between knowing truths and knowing things, has suggested to some philosophers that these represent two quite different ways of knowing, the one 'indirect' involving truths, and the other 'direct' where we seem to dispense with truths. Direct knowledge is then treated as primary and indirect knowledge as secondary. Direct knowledge, thought of by some philosophers as a sort of immediate confrontation with reality without the mediation of truths, is regarded as the paradigm of what knowledge should be: it has the merits of immediacy and incorrigibility. Indirect knowledge is a sort of substitute which we fall back on when direct knowledge is unavailable. Thus, it would be argued, since I did not come into contact with Caesar and did not have the opportunity of knowing him directly, I have to be content with knowing truths about him, such as that he was stabbed by Brutus, that he mistrusted Casca, etc. Or again, it is sometimes claimed that, in perception, I have immediate, direct knowledge of what is before my eyes or under my nose, for example I am in direct contact with the colour of the table when I look at it, with its hardness when I touch it, with the fragrance of the rose when I smell it. But of the table in the next room, it is added, I know only indirectly that it is round, that it is made of teak, etc. It is not surprising that those philosophers who favour this distinction have made it a central feature in their accounts of human knowledge: to them immediate confrontation with reality, i.e. direct knowledge, is the basis on which our knowledge of the world must be built.

On the other hand, it may well be argued that far too much has been made of this distinction and particularly that the claim that direct knowledge is able to dispense with knowledge of truths must be rejected. There may well be good reasons for contending that even knowing those things which are before my eyes involves knowledge of truths, for example knowing *that* this is a carpet, *that* it is blue, etc. Further, the difference between my knowledge of Caesar and that of his contemporaries may be explained merely in terms of the fact that they knew far more truths about him, that they had easier access to truths about him, that they were better placed to corroborate their views about him, and that the introduction of the epithet 'direct' does not refer to an alternative and superior way of knowing but merely to the fact that they, unlike me, had the pleasure of meeting him.

The distinction between knowledge of truths and knowing how to do something has also generated controversy. Sometimes these have been thought of as independent senses of knowledge and sometimes attempts have been made to reduce one to the other. If they are independent, is one primary and the other secondary? Should we think of knowledge primarily in terms of the possession of information or in terms of some skill or ability to do so-and-so?

The third distinction which has provided puzzlement is that based on the fact that in everyday life we sometimes use the word 'knowledge' rather rigorously, demanding that claims to knowledge should satisfy rigorous standards of proof, and at other times we are less severe and content ourselves with the production of evidence which settles some issue 'beyond reasonable doubt', but falls short of demonstrative proof. Thus, if someone claimed to know the truth of some geometrical proposition we would be inclined to ask for a proof. If, however, someone claimed that he knew who was responsible for setting fire to the Registry, we would accept evidence which identified the culprit 'beyond reasonable doubt'. Does this entail that there are two sorts of knowledge or two senses of 'knowledge', 'strong' and 'weak' knowledge, and should we conclude that only the strong variety really measures up to knowledge, so that 'weak' knowledge is called knowledge only by courtesy and should, if we wished to be precise, be described in other terms, as, for instance, belief or opinion? Or is so-called 'weak' knowledge what we ordinarily mean by knowledge, and should 'strong' knowledge be regarded as an oddity?

6   ORDINARY AND PHILOSOPHICAL SENSES OF 'KNOWLEDGE'

The last difficulties to be mentioned are raised by a consideration of the function of philosophy. One possibility is that there are confusions and even possibly mistakes in our everyday use of the term 'knowledge' which it is the business of philosophy to clear up. Should this be so, perhaps the confusion is to be eradicated by substituting some other concept, some technical philosophical concept, for that concept in everyday life which is deemed to be deficient. Thus many philosophers, alleging that our everyday use of the term 'knowledge' is muddled and confused, have sought to substitute such terms as 'apprehension', 'acquaintance' and 'rational assurance' in place of the familiar term 'knowledge'. The other possibility is that ordinary language can be defended against the charge of laxity and muddle, and that it can be shown that such philosophers, blinkered by a preconceived notion of what knowledge ought to be, have seen muddle and confusion where there is none. We must consider whether we should draw a line between seeking to make refinements to distinctions which are current and substituting a technical concept which may have little relevance to the concept for which it is substituted, and may even be in conflict with it. If the task of philosophy is to examine the concepts current in our everyday use of language with a view to widening our understanding of these familiar concepts themselves, we shall conclude that the imposition of a technical concept to replace the familiar one is unnecessary.

The purpose of this chapter has been limited to trying to exhibit to the reader who may be unacquainted with philosophical discussions about knowledge the range of problems involved. I have not sought to offer any answers, except in the restricted sense of seeking to convince such a reader that a simple definition of knowledge must inevitably fail to do justice to the almost bewildering complexity of the concept, and particularly to its intricate relationships with a number of other concepts. At the same time, I have suggested that the impact of philosophical speculation on the concept of knowledge might require us to revise many of our everyday assumptions about knowledge. I propose to tackle the traditional problems about knowledge by contrasting our everyday assumptions with some of the theories advanced by philosophers.

2 Everyday Assumptions about Knowledge

Many, if not most, of the concepts with which philosophers concern themselves are familiar before philosophical reflection on them begins. Concepts such as 'truth', 'reasoning', 'obligation', 'pleasure', 'society', 'freedom', for example, are extensively used in everyday life, and most people would claim familiarity with them. We do not, therefore, approach the study of philosophy with the expectation of learning about matters which were previously quite unfamiliar to us. Further, whereas we may approach the subject with the hope that our understanding of these familiar concepts may be broadened, we would, I think, be surprised if we were told at the start of our inquiry that we were to expect to find that our everyday understanding was radically mistaken. On the other hand, if we were approaching the study of physics, we would not be dismayed if we were told that we should be prepared for a radical alteration in our understanding of everyday concepts such as 'force' or 'energy'; nor would it surprise us to be warned that we were likely to be confronted with concepts which were quite unfamiliar in everyday life, such as 'entropy'.

A person unacquainted with philosophy might indeed concede that even the most familiar concepts might have features which he imperfectly understood or which he had not even noticed, and he might well concede further that there could be connections between familiar concepts of which he was unaware. He might not have realised, for example, the connection or lack of connection between the notions of 'truth' and 'validity' as drawn by logicians, or he might not have noticed that the notions of 'freedom' and 'obligation' are as closely connected as some philosophers insist they are. Such a person might therefore be mildly surprised if he were told that an argument could be valid even though the statements of which it were composed were not true, or that a condition of ascribing an obligation to someone was that the person concerned was free to do what the obligation prescribed. But the recruit to philosophy would, I suspect, be more than mildly surprised if he were informed by a philosopher that distinctions which were widely used in everyday life, and which he himself knew how to draw, had no validity and should be abandoned. What if, for example, he were told that although he claimed proficiency in distinguishing between those actions which he performed freely and those which he did not, the distinction between voluntary and involuntary action was illusory so that, in fact, none of his actions was freely performed? What if, again, he were told that although he claimed to have little or no difficulty in distinguishing between those actions of his which were physical, such as running, and those which were mental, such as imagining, the distinction between mental and physical actions was unreal, so that, in fact, all his actions were physical?

Surprise would surely give way to dismay if such a person was asked to accept that concepts with which he was quite familiar were entirely bogus or fictitious, for example if he were asked to accept that time was unreal or that a procedure as familiar as willing to do something simply did not and could not occur. Recruits to the study of philosophy must, indeed, as we shall see, be prepared for intellectual shocks of this kind.

One of the most familiar concepts in everyday life is that of knowledge. We all possess a good deal of it, and apart from unusual circumstances, we have little difficulty in deciding whether we, or anyone else, can be credited with knowledge in a particular case. Whether or not I know the atomic weight of tin, or whether you know the capital city of Peru, is something which can be ascertained with little difficulty. There are, no doubt, other situations where considerable investigation may be necessary before a decision on someone's claim to know may be reached: there may even be some situations where the decision has to be suspended until, perhaps, further evidence can be obtained. Although we must concede that we are not always in the happy position of being able to pronounce with authority on claims to knowledge, it would surely be an extraordinary event if someone were to try to persuade us that we were *never* in a position to do so, either on the grounds that our grasp of so familiar a concept as knowledge is so minimal that we are incapable of distinguishing it from other related concepts as belief, or on the grounds that knowledge in fact never occurs. To such a sceptic we might well reply that although we may not be familiar with every aspect of reasoning, we can at least recognise an argument when we meet one: even though we may lack logical sophistication we can often discover whether an argument is valid or not. Or we might reply that we can often determine the truth or falsity of a statement without knowing all that there is to know about 'truth', or that we can distinguish between pleasure and pain even though we are incapable of offering physiological explanations of them. Why, then, should we be in such a helpless position with regard to knowledge, a concept which is no less familiar than the rest?

I do not wish to suggest to those uninitiated in philosophy that it is the standard practice of philosophers to advance doctrines as remote from common sense as the doctrine that we are incapable of distinguishing between knowledge and belief, or the doctrine that knowledge never occurs, though, indeed, these doctrines have been advanced from time to time. It must, however, be admitted that most, if not all, of the assumptions about knowledge which we make in everyday life have been challenged at one time or another by philosophers. The purpose of this book is to examine the reasons which have been advanced for questioning our everyday assumptions with a view to seeing how many of them survive the onslaughts of theorists about knowledge. I propose, therefore, to list and examine briefly the assumptions about knowledge which, in my view, are widely held and, at the same time, to mention some of the philosophical doctrines which appear to be in conflict with them.

1. We do not normally restrict the application of the term 'knowledge' to any special subject matter. On the contrary, we are quite prepared to concede that people may obtain knowledge in a very wide range of subjects. Thus we would accept that claims to knowledge can reasonably be made about all sorts of propositions: we are prepared to consider claims to know the truth of mathematical, economic, scientific and historical propositions, among others, quite apart from the endless variety of propositions

of a non-technical nature related to everyday experience, such as my knowing that it rained in Cardiff yesterday, that the Derby is run at Epsom in June, that the desk at which I am now sitting is made of wood, etc. This is not, of course, to say that we allow that knowledge is obtainable in every sphere. Thus we would be reluctant to admit that long range weather forecasting could aspire to be classified as knowledge, though we might well concede the possibility that it might do so in the future. Knowledge, in this case, we might say, is in practice impossible at the present time, though it is not impossible in principle. On the other hand, some might say, and indeed have said, that there are other matters which in principle cannot be known, for example that God exists or that the soul is immortal or propositions about the remote future. We seem to distinguish, therefore, between those categories of things which can be known, those which in practice cannot now be known and those which in principle never could be. The category of things which can be known is, so we ordinarily believe, a very wide one: what we appear never to contemplate is the possibility that everything is in principle unknowable.

When we turn to the writings of theorists about knowledge we find that it has frequently been contended that the possibility of achieving knowledge is much more restricted than we normally suppose. One such contention is that knowledge is obtainable only in such disciplines as mathematics and logic. Other disciplines, such as history and natural science, are for ever debarred from achieving knowledge, and the alleged certainties of everyday life are relegated to the status of beliefs or probabilities. Sometimes this contention is based on the distinction, familiar in everyday life, between those things which could have been otherwise and those which could not. For instance, philosophers have noticed that whereas the occurrence of the Battle of Waterloo in 1815 was an accidental or contingent happening which might have been otherwise, the fact that two and two make four or that Mr X, if a bachelor, must be unmarried, could not be otherwise. Having noticed this distinction between what they sometimes describe as 'contingent' and 'necessary' truths, some philosophers have proceeded to restrict the possibility of achieving knowledge to necessary truths, of which mathematics and logic are said to be composed. From this it follows that propositions which are only contingently true, those of history, for example, could never be possible objects of knowledge, but must remain in perpetuity as objects of belief. I must, therefore, never claim to know that it rained in Cardiff yesterday, that oak trees shed their leaves in the autumn, that my opponent holed his tee shot in one at the 12th last Saturday, solely on the grounds that none of these events could be classified as 'necessary'. The widespread practice of claiming to know the truth of propositions outside the realm of 'necessary truths', so such philosophers recommend, is just a mistake and should be discontinued.

At other times the restriction on the application of the term 'knowledge' is based on the distinction between those features of the world which are alleged to be constant and unchanging and those features of the world which are subject to change and decay. Thus it has been claimed by philosophers from the earliest times to the present day that everything which we experience in sense perception is constantly changing: we never see the same river twice; one's friends and acquaintances age; familiar objects such as desks, carpets, castles and pennies take on different appearances depending on the light conditions etc. From considerations such as these, the conclusion has been drawn that nothing which is subject to change can be known; it is assumed or presupposed that a condition of the possibility of knowledge is that its 'objects' should be permanent. Knowledge must, therefore, be confined to the eternal and unchanging, and the quest for knowledge, for philosophers who take this view, has been the quest for eternal and unchanging entities which alone can serve as the proper objects of knowledge. Admitting that particular true statements such as 'It is raining now' may be true now and false later, they assert that 'truth' itself never alters: admitting that particular beautiful objects may appear beautiful to me and ugly to you and may even lose their beauty altogether, they assert that 'beauty' itself is eternal. Should we, of course, not be able to identify things which do not change, the conclusion would have to be drawn, given these premisses, that knowledge of anything is impossible.

There are, no doubt, a variety of reasons why so many philosophers have adopted this restrictive attitude to the range of things which can be known. I have mentioned two considerations which have influenced philosophers, namely the conviction that there is an essential link between the concepts of knowledge and necessity, in the sense that only propositions which are necessarily true can be known, and the complementary conviction that there is an essential link between the concepts of knowledge and

permanence, in the sense that only those things which are change-
less can be proper objects of knowledge. But the overriding
reason, the development and criticism of which is one of the
central themes in this book, is the desire to protect knowledge
from even the theoretical possibility of error. It is not enough, it is
alleged, that what is known *is*, in fact, true; it must be *impossible* for
it to be false. In order to be right about something, there must not
be the chance of being wrong. This view is sometimes expressed in
the form that knowledge must be 'infallible' or 'incorrigible'. One
of the ways in which knowledge could be immunised against the
risk of error, it was thought, was by restricting the range of things
which could be known to propositions which could not in any
circumstances be false, for example 'Two and two make four', 'If
A is bigger than B and B is bigger than C, then A is bigger than C'.
On the other hand, I should not claim to know that the coal
bucket is empty solely on the grounds that the proposition 'The
coal bucket is empty' *could* be false. This restriction was sometimes
coupled with and facilitated by the distinction drawn from Plato
onwards between 'sensation' and 'reason' as possible sources of
knowledge. The widespread distrust of sensation or perception,
based on its alleged liability to error, left the field open for reason,
said to be concerned with propositions which could not be false, as
the sole source of knowledge. Perception is then relegated to the
secondary realm of belief. The picture is completed by identifying
the sphere of perception with what is changing and the sphere of
reason with what is permanent.

2. A further important assumption which we normally make is
that, while allowing that knowledge may be obtained in a wide
variety of subjects, we do not expect that knowledge claims in all
subject matters should be justified in the same way. We allow that
the reasons which a man may offer to justify his knowledge claims
will vary from one type of proposition to another. Thus, if
someone claims to know the sum of 6284 and 5432, he will try to
justify his claim in one way; if he claims to know what Caesar said
when he crossed the Rubicon, he will try to justify his claim in
another way: if he claims to know that chlorine will expand if
heated, he will try to justify his claim in yet another way. We do
not believe that God has been so sparing to men that he has given
them only one method for justifying everything. Further, we do
not, in everyday life, single out any one method of justifying
knowledge claims as vastly superior to all other accredited

methods. We listen with equal attention and respect to the claims of barristers, historians, botanists and economists, and it would occasion considerable surprise in non-mathematical or non-logical circles if the claim were made that mathematicians and logicians were endowed with methods which were far superior to those of all other practitioners. In other words, we realise that there are many different types of problems, that there are many methods suitable for their solution, and that a method adapted to solve one type of problem is powerless to solve problems of a different type. Geometrical methods of proof, for example, cannot be used to solve historical problems, nor can historical methods solve problems in chemistry. What is abundantly clear is that we do not assume that only mathematical or logical problems are soluble, or that problems in chemistry are insoluble because they are not amenable to geometrical methods of proof. The adoption of a respectful attitude to mathematicians does not require us to be suspicious of, say, botanists and geographers.

Traditionally, the word 'proof' has been used to refer to any accredited method of justification, so that we could speak of theological proofs, historical proofs, scientific proofs, or indeed more generally of any procedure of establishing a fact. This well attested usage where 'to prove' is equivalent to demonstrating the truth of anything by evidence or by argument has tended to be supplanted by a technical sense of the term applied, for instance, in arithmetic where it is equivalent to checking the correctness of a calculation. More generally, 'to prove' has been assimilated to that method of argument which logicians describe as 'deduction', i.e. a type of argument which is such that if the premisses are true, the conclusion, if validly drawn, must also be true. Arguments of this type, so it is claimed, at least in their pure form, are more or less restricted to logic and mathematics. The step has been taken of asserting that deduction is the only method of argument which measures up to the rigorous standards required for knowledge. Having set up deduction as the paradigm, it has been relatively easy to conclude that any other method of proof whose credentials fall short of those of deduction is in principle untrustworthy. The methods employed by natural scientists, lawyers, historians, social scientists, etc. (in so far as they do not consist of pure deduction) are grouped together under the title of 'inductive methods', i.e. arguments such that even though the premisses are true, the conclusions may be false. Such methods, misleadingly grouped together as 'inductive', are condemned only to produce, at the best, belief. This general thesis would, I suspect, appear less plausible if it were expressed in the form that it is only mathematicians and logicians who are fortunate enough to be concerned with problems which are soluble. Chemists, one fears, would not gladly accept the suggestion that the problem of the chemical composition of Penicillin, which greatly exercised them some years ago, was not in a strict sense soluble.

We see here again, I believe, the same motive of wishing to protect knowledge at all costs from the possible intrusion of error, this time by restricting the possible achievement of knowledge to a method of argument which is thought to be foolproof.

3. We do not in everyday life take the view that some propositions are intrinsically 'known' or 'knowable' and others intrinsically 'believed' or 'believable'. We allow that a proposition which is believed to be true by me may be known to be true by you or *vice versa*. Thus I may be reluctant to claim that I know that the Battle of Waterloo was fought in 1815, and content myself with the more modest attitude of belief. You, on the other hand, may claim to know that it was fought in 1815, and may be able to make good your claim to know it. I may believe that sulphurous acid is a mixture of sulphur dioxide and water: you may know it and be able to give a convincing account of its composition. The same applies even to mathematical propositions. If you set me a sum which involves more than a little mathematical manipulation, I might well have little confidence in the correctness of my answer. Someone else, more adept at mathematical calculation, could work it out with conviction that his answer was correct and be able to demonstrate it. We should, therefore, beware of the superficially plausible view that mathematical propositions, for instance, are intrinsically 'knowable'.

It is surely clear, in the first place, that the question whether a given proposition is known or knowable is elliptical and must be filled out by the addition of 'known by someone or other'. Being 'knowable' or 'believable' is not a possible adjective which we can apply to propositions in themselves. The question whether a proposition is known or knowable only arises when someone claims to know it. It should also be clear, in the second place, that if someone claims to know that a given proposition is true, the only way in which the matter can be settled is by an investigation of the reasons which he offers to support his claim to know. What cannot, surely, be true is the suggestion that simple inspection of a proposition would enable us to determine whether it is known or knowable or just believed or believable. Thus, the proposition that Waterloo was fought in 1815 does not in itself give any clue as to whether it is known or believed, and no inspection of the proposition *in abstracto*, however prolonged, will reveal its secret status. Whether or not a given individual knows it or merely believes it can be settled only by investigating the reasons which he advances. 'Being knowable' is not the natural prerogative of a proposition. I am here disregarding tautologies (e.g. 'A book is a book') and contradictions (e.g. 'This is a round square'), where it might be claimed that simple inspection would assure us of their truth and falsity respectively.

As against this, the claim has often been advanced that it is of the nature of some things, for example so-called 'universals' such as 'truth', 'beauty', 'goodness', and of the nature of some propositions to be either 'knowable' or 'believable'. For instance, the propositions of logic and mathematics are said to be intrinsically 'knowable', whereas the propositions of history, by contrast, or indeed of any subject which relies to any degree on perception, are intrinsically 'believable'. Propositions which can be classified as 'necessarily true' fall into the former category: those classified as 'contingently true' fall into the latter. Its 'knowability' is regarded as a feature of the proposition in itself, and is not held to be dependent on its being known by anybody or on the reasons which someone might advance in support of a claim to know it. The frontier between propositions which are 'knowable' and those which are 'believable' cannot, it seems, be crossed. It would not, therefore, be possible on this view for you to know the truth of a proposition such as 'The Battle of Waterloo was fought in 1815' (a proposition described as inherently believable) and for me to believe it.

4. In everyday speech we do not allow the possibility of using the verb 'to know' in such a way that, if someone knows that a proposition is true, the given proposition could be false, i.e. if someone knows p, then p is true. If I know that the atomic weight of lead is 207·2, then it must be 207·2. However, we are not prepared to concede that a man knows something simply because he claims to know it. On the contrary, we are familiar with knowledge claims which turn out on investigation to be unjustified. The mere fact of saying 'I know' does not guarantee

acceptance of the claim. We are all aware that in the process of getting to know something or other, we may well go astray and fall into error rather than achieve knowledge. We saw earlier that we do not assume that the accredited methods of historians or chemists or botanists are inherently doomed to failure: it is relevant at this point to emphasise that we do not regard any methods of discovery as inherently guaranteeing success. We naturally expect that if someone claims to know something, he should be in a position to justify his claim, and we are rightly suspicious of claims to knowledge which the claimant regards as self-justifying. Indeed, we adopt the same attitude to claims of any sort: no-one will accept my claim to be the longest driver of a golf ball in Wales simply because I make it, or my claim that the treasure which someone has found is mine because I say so.

It is, surely, one of the most obvious features of human activity in all its aspects that it is subject to failure as well as success. Travellers do not have to arrive at their destinations; I am not bound to find my missing pen — indeed, we may fail to reach our goal in anything we seek to do. It is not so much that procedures which inherently guarantee success are beyond our finite reach, such as searching which *must* result in finding or travelling which *must* result in arriving; we could attach no meaning to the introduction of such notions. Similarly, we recognise that the methods by means of which men have acquired knowledge such as observing, experimenting, inferring, calculating, etc. are not bound to result in success. In spite of these considerations, many philosophers, as well as some laymen, have asserted that there can be knowledge claims which require no justification on the grounds that their success is self-guaranteed. Sometimes the familiar term 'intuition' has been drafted to assume the role of an incorrigible way of knowing, with or without the addition of the epithet 'rational'. Sometimes terms, familiar in other contexts, have been pressed into service in a similar capacity, for example 'acquaintance' or 'apprehension'. Thus for many philosophers the paradigm of knowledge is not the discovery of some fact after patient study which might have gone astray, getting something right where we might have got it wrong: it is the occurrence of instantaneous events, such as acts of intuition or acquaintance, which have only to occur for their success to be guaranteed. Into this category fall, for instance, Descartes's intuition of his own existence or Russell's acquaintance with the colour of the desk in perception or one's own mental states in introspection.

This attitude to the concept of knowledge, I suggest, is again motivated by the desire to safeguard its inviolability. Where, previously, this was attempted by restricting the range of things which can be known, it is now attempted by confining knowing to those procedures which are alleged to be self-justifying or self-guaranteeing.

5. On the other hand, the acceptance of the fact that attempts to get to know something are liable to go astray does not lead us to assume that the most dire consequences must follow. From the fact that we sometimes get things wrong, we do not conclude that we can never get things right; we certainly do not contemplate the possibility that we can know nothing whatsoever, that we are bound to be wrong about everything. On the contrary, we assume that if there is the possibility of getting things wrong, there must also be the possibility of getting things right. Procedures of falsification are possible only because there are also procedures of confirmation. The notion of searching which *never* could result in finding is as absurd as the notion of searching which *must* result in finding. From the fact that trains sometimes collide and fail to reach their destinations we do not pessimistically infer that railway transport is intrinsically so fallible that no trains ever could reach their destinations.

As previously noticed, we distinguish in everyday life between knowledge and related concepts such as belief and opinion. Thus we admit that what a person believes may be false and may be true, whereas what a person knows can only be true. We do not just equate the two concepts of knowledge and belief. Sometimes, in seeking to distinguish between knowledge and belief, we insist on a high degree of rigour before conceding a claim to knowledge. This insistence depends very largely on the special circumstances or on the particular subject matter of the claim. We require lawyers and professional historians, for instance, to satisfy rigorous standards of proof. But we are not always very demanding, for example, if our neighbour claims to know which horse won the Derby in 1920. Although we may vary our criteria, we never insist on such impossibly rigorous standards of proof that claims to knowledge could *never* satisfy them. High standards in any sphere of life may well be a meritorious aspiration, but standards which in principle could never be attained are no standards at all.

Whereas in the previous section we noticed that there are some philosophers who advocate the view that there are self-justifying ways of knowing, we now find that there are other philosophers who despair of the possibility of ever acquiring knowledge at all, apart from knowledge of propositions of a relatively trivial nature. Such propositions, often described as 'analytic', are variously defined as 'propositions true solely in terms of the meanings of the words' or as 'terminological recommendations for the use of words', for example 'A book is a book', 'If X is a bachelor, he is unmarried'. Apart from such propositions, some philosophers have insisted upon such high standards for so-called empirical knowledge (i.e. knowledge of facts as opposed to knowledge of the meanings of words), that their satisfaction can never be achieved. Knowledge of matters of fact is thus declared to be impossible. But in everyday life we do not dismiss the knowledge claims of historians or lawyers or botanists without a hearing on the grounds that we are assured that they could never achieve the stringent standards required for knowledge of matters of fact.

6. Although we are familiar with the experience of knowing that so-and-so is the case and equally familiar with the experience of believing that so-and-so is the case, we do not assume that a simple process of self-examination would enable us to distinguish conclusively between knowing and believing in a particular situation. The experience of knowing, if, indeed, it is an experience, is not something which identifies itself. On the contrary, we are only too aware of the danger of mistaking knowledge for error, i.e. thinking that we know a proposition to be true when in fact it is false. Psychologically, error and knowledge, as states of mind, are indistinguishable: for instance, both the person who knows and the person who thinks he knows but is in error are free from doubt, or, as it is sometimes expressed, both are equally confident of the truth of what they assert. Indeed, one of the most insidious features of error is its success in simulating knowledge. If someone claims to know a fact, our cross-examination of him does not take the form of asking him to pronounce on his state of mind. We require him, usually at least, to produce reasons or evidence in support of his claim, and we attach more weight to the reasons which he advances than to his autobiographical reports. We could, indeed, dispense with tedious processes of investigating reasons and weighing evidence if a simple inspection of one's state of mind were an adequate test of knowledge. Nor would it be plausible to claim that, although the above account may be true of

other people's claims to knowledge, it cannot be true of mine, that is, that other people's claims need investigation while mine need none. We would, indeed, reach an impasse if it were true that each person could be sure of his own bits of knowledge and everybody was unsure of everybody else's. Just as my claims to be generous or intelligent are as much open to your scrutiny as your claims are to mine, so my claims to knowledge are exactly on a par with yours. I am not suggesting that this parity need necessarily always be the case; it might well be that my claim to have a headache or to be hungry is not subject to your scrutiny. But that it is true of claims to being generous or intelligent or having knowledge is surely manifest.

This everyday assumption that knowledge is not something which identifies itself, so that simple inspection of one's state of mind will not settle the question whether we are knowing or not, has, in fact, frequently been challenged by philosophers. The claim has been made, for example, that whenever we know something we either do, or at least can, directly know by simple inspection that we are knowing it, and also that whenever we believe something we can similarly know that we are believing it and not knowing it. Knowing is then conceived of as an unique and unanalysable experience, the mere occurrence of which cannot be mis-identified by its owner.

The following, then, in brief are some of the assumptions about knowledge which I believe to be widely held in everyday life and which philosophers have challenged from time to time:

1. There is, in general, no restriction on the range of subjects about which knowledge is possible.

2. There is not just one single method of justification or proof of claims to knowledge.

3. Propositions are not to be classified as intrinsically 'knowable' or 'believable'.

4. There are no self-guaranteeing or 'incorrigible' ways of knowing.

5. It is pointless to set standards of proof so high that their achievement is in principle impossible.

6. Knowledge and related concepts such as belief and opinion cannot be distinguished simply by self-examination of one's state of mind.

My own view is that the assumptions which I have listed are justified, and that they have been challenged only because of the acceptance on the part of some philosophers of some or all of the following myths:

1. Knowledge must be infallible, in the sense that for something to count as knowledge, there must not even be the theoretical possibility of mistake.

2. A consequence of (1) is that knowledge must be accorded separate 'objects' from other cognitive attitudes, especially belief. Otherwise, the infallibility of knowledge is threatened.

3. Knowing is a sort of mental act, something which we *do*, comparable with thinking, inferring, perceiving, etc. Particularly when linked with (1), knowing is regarded as a kind of infallible act, best exemplified in intuition and acquaintance.

4. Knowing as a mental act or state is intimately connected with conviction or 'being sure'. If knowing and being sure cannot be identified, then being sure is at least a necessary condition of knowing.

5. Knowing as an infallible act must be self-certifying. We cannot know without knowing that we know, just as we cannot have pains without being aware of them.

A consequence of the acceptance of some or all of the above myths is that we are liable to misunderstand the relationship between knowledge and belief. Many philosophers, it is true, have rejected both (1) and (2). But many who have done so have gone to the other extreme and concluded that there is no radical difference between knowledge and belief. Having subsumed knowledge under belief, they are faced with the impossible task of looking for the 'necessary conditions' for distinguishing that belief which is knowledge from that belief which is not.

In subsequent chapters I shall try to defend the above everyday assumptions against what I regard as the mistaken theories which oppose them. The primary myth, from which most of the others are derived, is (1), and priority must be given to its eradication.

3 Knowledge and Infallibility

One of the recurring themes in the history of speculation about knowledge is the notion that knowledge cannot be mistaken. At first sight this would appear to be platitudinously true. There would, I expect, be general agreement that there cannot be two varieties of knowledge, namely true knowledge and false knowledge, as there are two varieties of belief, namely true belief and false belief. If, therefore, the dictum 'knowledge cannot be mistaken' implies no more than the fact that the disjunction 'either true or false' does not apply to knowledge, there is no problem: if someone believes that a given proposition is true, the proposition may be true and may be false; if, however, someone knows that a given proposition is true, then the proposition *is* true. In this sense, knowledge and truth are inextricably linked in a way in which belief and truth are not.

We should, however, notice immediately that the dictum 'knowledge cannot be mistaken' does not in itself make any stipulations about the status of the proposition which is known to be true, nor does it stipulate any special procedures by means of which this item of knowledge is to be acquired. Thus it is quite consistent with the dictum that knowledge cannot be mistaken to cite any type of proposition to fill the place of *p* in 'Someone knows that *p* is true'. To comply with the dictum we could equally well cite as examples 'Someone knows that two and two make four' or 'Someone knows that this desk is made of wood', or 'Someone knows that Waterloo was fought in 1815', provided only that it is true that two and two make four, that the desk is made of wood and that Waterloo was fought in 1815. To anticipate difficulties, we should point out at this stage that we might not be prepared to accept someone's claim to know such propositions as those listed above solely on the grounds that the propositions in question are true. We might, for example, reject claims to know them if we had reason to suspect that the claimant had stumbled upon the truth of these propositions by accident or by guessing, i.e. the fact that the proposition which a person claims to know to be true *is* true does not in itself prove that he knows it. Being right by accident, we ordinarily suppose, will not count as knowledge. For this reason philosophers have stipulated other conditions, for example that the claimant must be sure or that he must be able to justify his claim by the production of suitable evidence or by argument. The consideration of what extra conditions must be introduced is, of course, essential for a full understanding of what is implied by saying that someone knows that a given proposition is true. But such a consideration is not strictly relevant to an investigation of what is implied by the dictum 'knowledge cannot be mistaken' on the minimal interpretation which we have accepted as a truism. The dictum requires only that the proposition in question should be true.

We should notice, secondly, that the fact that the dictum does not restrict us to any particular type of proposition in our choice of examples of the sorts of things which people can be said to know is entirely in line with our everyday use of the term 'knowledge'. We show no reluctance to say that someone knows that Sir Francis Drake was buried at sea, or that someone knows that oxygen will expand if heated, or that someone knows that St Paul's Cathedral is in the city of London, or that someone knows that the carpet in his room is black, etc. That is, in order to satisfy the requirements of the minimal interpretation of the dictum we are not obliged to isolate any one type of proposition, for example a proposition from mathematics, and insist that only propositions of that type can be used to complete statements of the form 'Someone knows that p is true'.

We should notice, in the third place, that compliance with the requirements of the dictum does not necessarily restrict the methods by means of which a given item of knowledge is acquired. There is, of course, a variety of ways in which we discover the truth of the propositions which we claim to know. To the question 'How did you discover that p is true?' there is no one standard answer. Thus I may have come to know that Drake was buried at sea by hearsay: I may have come to know that oxygen expands when heated by witnessing an experiment in the laboratory: I may have come to know the topography of St Paul's by browsing in a reference book. Some truths I learn as the result of inference, while often I dispense with inference. So far as compliance with the requirement that knowledge cannot be mistaken is concerned, we are not unduly impressed by sceptical persons who point out that not everything which we learn by hearsay is correct, that experimenters have been known to slip up and unwittingly substitute chlorine for oxygen, that reference books frequently contain mistakes, that slips are always possible in conducting inferences, etc. Sceptical arguments of this sort may well be relevant in other contexts, for instance they may be relevant to determining whether someone can be credited with knowing that something is true on a particular occasion, i.e. they may be relevant to establishing the claim to knowledge made by someone at a particular time. But they are not relevant so far as the satisfaction of the dictum 'knowledge cannot be mistaken' is concerned. To repeat: the minimal interpretation requires only that where someone knows that a proposition is true, the proposition *is* true, and is itself indifferent both to the type of proposition in question and to the method of its discovery.

Philosophers, however, have not always been content with this minimal interpretation of the dictum. It has been interpreted in a variety of ways, some of which involve far more than the obvious, though important, point mentioned above. Examples of such extended interpretations are: 'knowledge must be infallible', 'knowledge must be incorrigible', 'knowledge must be absolute'. I propose to consider now the implications of the frequently held view that knowledge must be infallible or incorrigible, expressions which I shall regard as roughly synonymous.

It is not always clear whether those philosophers who wish to introduce the notions of infallibility or incorrigibility in relation to knowledge regard these alleged characteristics as relating primarily to the nature of the propositions which it is possible to know, or to the procedures by means of which items of knowledge can be acquired. Sometimes the emphasis is on the former, sometimes on the latter, and sometimes on both. In either case, it is clear that the promotion of 'knowledge cannot be mistaken' to mean 'knowledge must be infallible or incorrigible' will impose the most severe restrictions both on the range of things which can be known and on the range of procedures which can yield knowledge. Thus it will not now be enough that the proposition which a person knows *is* true: it must further be added that a condition of the possibility of knowledge is that it should be impossible for the proposition to be false. With regard to the procedures which may yield knowledge, corresponding restrictions have to be imposed. In order to satisfy the dictum 'knowledge must be infallible', any procedure which involves the possibility of error has to be excluded. Thus of the examples mentioned earlier as examples of the sorts of things which, in everyday life, we would be prepared to say that people could know, none would satisfy the new requirements. We can no longer say that I know that Sir Francis Drake was buried at sea because the method by which I learnt this is 'fallible': hearsay is not an absolutely reliable, fault-free method of discovery. Nor can I say that I know that the carpet in my room is black since observation is not a totally reliable source of knowledge. Nor can I say that I know that oxygen will expand if heated since, apart from the fact this discovery too would depend partly on suspect observation, all sorts of things might have gone wrong when the experiment was conducted. Further, maps and reference books are not immune from mistakes. The only procedures which can yield knowledge, we shall have to conclude, are those procedures which are self-guaranteeing or self-justifying, in the sense that the possibility of error is necessarily excluded. If knowledge is to be possible, there will have to be, on such a view as this, incorrigible ways of knowing as well as incorrigible propositions, i.e. risk-free methods of discovery as well as propositions which in no circumstances could be false. Should we fail to find either, the only possible conclusion to be drawn would be that knowledge is impossible. Our task is to see whether this dreary conclusion can be avoided.

The question which, I think, must constantly be borne in mind is whether this extension of the innocuous dictum 'knowledge cannot be mistaken' to 'knowledge must be infallible' is required in order to understand our everyday use of the concept of knowledge, or whether, on the other hand, this extension is due to misconceptions on the part of philosophers with the result that it actually distorts our everyday concept of knowledge. It might be prudent to remember that the concept of knowledge is not one which is proprietary to philosophers: it is equally in the ownership of barristers, historians, scientists, road-sweepers, etc. It might also be salutary to ask ourselves what would be gained and who would gain by inventing a concept of knowledge which fits in with philosophical theories at the expense of being out of touch with our customary understanding of the concept.

We must now examine further some of the many versions of the doctrine that knowledge must be infallible. Of those available, the following seem to be the most widely supported:

1. On this view, the possibility of knowledge is restricted to propositions which have the characteristic of being 'necessarily true'. This special status of the propositions which can be known is thought to rule out the possibility of error. Thus propositions which happen to be true but could have been false, such as 'It is raining', do not qualify as possible 'objects' of knowledge. If the things which I can know could not in any circumstances be false, there is no chance of knowledge being mistaken, it is thought. Usually, on this view, the propositions which satisfy the requirement of being necessarily true are the so-called 'analytic' propositions to which reference has already been made. Such propositions have been variously described as propositions which are true solely in terms of the meanings of the words employed, or propositions which are true by definition, or propositions the denial of which would produce a self-contradiction. Examples of such propositions are usually drawn from mathematics and logic, for instance 'Two and two make four' and 'If A is bigger than B and B is bigger than C, then A is bigger than C', together with trivial propositions such as 'A book is a book'. It does not, of course, follow from the fact that a given proposition is necessarily true that I know it or that anyone else knows it. For example, on the given definitions of a necessary truth, any mathematical proposition would be necessarily true, but there are, of course, endless mathematical propositions of which any particular individual is ignorant. There may also be many necessary truths of which I can claim only that I believe them to be true. This view cannot, then, be committing us to saying that any necessary truth must be known, but only to saying that the only propositions which can be known are necessarily true propositions. The acceptance of the view, in these terms, entails that no factual proposition based on observation, such as 'The coal bucket is empty', could ever qualify as a candidate for being an object of knowledge.

It has sometimes been suggested that this view can be disproved simply by showing that it is based on a confusion. It is, so it is said, plausible only because of the ambiguity in the expression

'If someone knows p, then p *must* be true', and there is no justification for the jump which may unwittingly have been taken of arguing that since p must be true, then p must be a necessarily true proposition. As we saw earlier, the dictum that knowledge cannot be mistaken does not require that the proposition which is known to be true should be of any special status: it requires only that it *is* true. Certainly the jump from saying 'If someone knows p, then p must be true' (where this merely entails that p *is* true) to saying that p must be true in the sense that it entails that p must be a necessarily true proposition, is unjustified as it stands: it would not in itself disqualify other propositions, for instance contingently true propositions, from being possible objects of knowledge. But the mere exposure of this ambiguity is not, I suggest, enough to discredit the view that knowledge must be infallible; it must be supplemented by dispelling the idea that knowledge must at all costs be safeguarded from the possibility of error, which is the main motive for accepting the doctrine. What we should, I think, say when confronted with such a view as this, is that we do not in everyday life restrict the possibility of knowledge to necessarily true propositions, and that before we abandon our customary practice, we require positive arguments to show that propositions which are only contingently true, i.e. which *are* true but *could* have been false, cannot in any circumstances be known.

2. The second version of the doctrine that knowledge implies infallibility does not restrict the possibility of knowledge to necessarily true propositions. On this view, it is possible to allow a wider range of propositions, including contingently true propositions, the denial of which does not produce a self-contradiction. But only a restricted range of such factual propositions can be accommodated, namely propositions which 'describe my immediate experiences'. Such propositions are commonly thought to be of two kinds, namely (a) propositions which describe my immediate perceptual experiences, and (b) propositions which describe my present sensations or feelings. There is, however, considerable dispute over the interpretation of (a). The more generous interpretation allows that propositions involving material things can count as propositions which can be known and about which I cannot be mistaken, for example such a proposition as 'This is a desk', when uttered by me in the presence of the desk. On the narrower interpretation, reference to material things, such as desks, castles, books, etc., must be excluded for a variety of

reasons and especially on the grounds that the introduction of material things allows the possibility of error. This is so, it is claimed, because material things are not what we are 'directly aware of': reference to them involves straying far beyond what is actually 'given' in perception. We must, therefore, express ourselves solely in terms of the things with which we are directly acquainted, or in terms of the things which are actually given, namely the colour, shape, hardness, etc. which constitute the 'appearance' of the desk. The description of our immediate perceptual experiences in terms of such 'sense-data', as they are frequently called, rather than in terms of material things, is said to have two advantages. First, it is a more accurate description of what we 'actually perceive', and secondly, and more importantly in the present context, it exempts us from the risk of error.

The other type of proposition which is often claimed to be infallible or incorrigible is that in which we describe the content of our present sensations or feelings. Thus of such propositions as 'I am feeling tired' and 'I have an ache' it is claimed that the person asserting them cannot possibly be mistaken, so that they are examples of propositions which we can be said to know.

3. The third version of the doctrine that knowledge implies infallibility is concerned not so much with the attempt to discover propositions which are incorrigible as to identify methods of knowing which in themselves eliminate the risk of error. Examples of such ways of knowing are alleged to be 'intuition' and 'acquaintance', which are represented as 'direct' and infallible ways of knowing. Sometimes the propositions which we are said to be able to intuit are necessarily true propositions or self-evidently true propositions: in this case this version joins forces with the first version of the thesis that knowledge implies infallibility. But at other times propositions of a more doubtful character are included, such as Descartes' primary intuition of his own existence, expressed as 'Cogito ergo sum'.

The notion of 'acquaintance' as a kind of knowing which is incorrigible or infallible differs in many respects from that of intuition. The main difference, at least for our present purposes, is that, whereas intuition is said to be directed to truths or facts, acquaintance is said to be directed to things, and also to objects which are not regarded as things, such as persons. Thus a sharp distinction is drawn between our knowledge of things and our knowledge of truths. Knowledge of things, it is claimed, is logically independent of knowledge of truths, even though in practice it may seldom, if ever, occur without some knowledge of truths being present. The other important feature of acquaintance, which it is thought to share with intuition, is that it dispenses with inference. Both are, in this respect, 'direct' or 'immediate'. The things with which I have acquaintance, according to one exponent of the doctrine, namely Russell, are the sense-data with which I am directly confronted in perception, for example the colour, shape and hardness of the desk, but not the desk itself. Secondly, the things which we have previously seen, heard, etc. are immediately present to us in memory. Thirdly, we can be directly aware of or acquainted with our own mental states in introspection, for example when I desire food, I can be acquainted with my desire for food. Lastly, we can have acquaintance with 'universals', i.e. general ideas such as whiteness, diversity, brotherhood, etc. (Russell's doctrine of acquaintance will be discussed in detail in Chapter 7.) It should be noticed that both the advocates of intuition and of acquaintance conceive of knowledge as some sort of instantaneous act, as a confrontation with or discovery of a fact or truth or thing.

4. A recent version of the doctrine that knowledge implies infallibility has been developed by Professor R. I. Aaron in *Knowing and the Function of Reason* (Oxford: The Clarendon Press, 1971). On this view, it is legitimate to talk about the possibility of knowledge, which is certain and complete, in a wide variety of circumstances. Thus I may legitimately claim to know that I am here at this moment, that my friend is sitting opposite me, that there is a table there, etc. Such knowledge, though properly described as certain and complete, yet remains 'fallible', and must be contrasted with knowledge which is both certain and infallible. A distinction is drawn between certainty and infallibility. This view does not require that there should be instances of 'absolute', 'infallible' knowledge: it requires only that the notion of knowledge as absolute and infallible must be retained as an ideal which can be conceived though never attained. On this view, therefore, we are able to admit that there are many sorts of factual propositions derived from experience which can be known, though such knowledge has to be described as 'fallible'. The merits of such a version of the infallibility doctrine, it may well be thought, are that it does not restrict knowledge to the narrow range of necessarily true propositions, nor are we required to invoke special

instantaneous procedures such as intuition and acquaintance.

The one feature which is common to all versions of the doctrine that knowledge implies infallibility is that, in order for the concept of knowledge to be applicable, there must not be the possibility of error. It is this feature which distinguishes the thesis that knowledge must be infallible from the minimal interpretation of the earlier dictum that knowledge cannot be mistaken, which we accepted as a truism. It is the difference between saying that where someone knows p, p is true but could have been false, and saying that where someone knows p, p is true and could not have been false. There is also the corresponding difference between a method of discovery which in this case is successful but which might have been unsuccessful, and a method which in principle could only be successful. Before considering whether the doctrine of infallibility is inconsistent with or is required by our ordinary understanding of the concept of knowledge, I should like to indicate some of the general considerations which have influenced upholders of the doctrine.

Historically, the chief influence, I think, has been the model of knowledge derived from Plato. Knowledge is conceived as some sort of immediate confrontation with what is 'real', so that the degree to which something is 'real' will determine the degree to which it is knowable. The further step is taken of identifying what is 'real' with what is permanent or unchanging: hence the conclusion that for knowledge to be possible it must be concerned with 'objects' that cannot change. Translated into propositional terms, this becomes the thesis that knowledge must be restricted to propositions which in no circumstances could be false, i.e. to propositions which are necessarily true. Plato seems to have considered that it is only by restricting knowledge to what is 'real' (which, in the modern idiom, I interpret as equivalent to restricting knowledge to propositions which are necessarily true) that it would be possible to distinguish between knowledge and belief, a distinction which was central to his theory of knowledge. The opposition between knowledge and belief, as an opposition between an infallible and a fallible state of mind, required that there should be a radical difference between their 'objects': the objects of knowledge would be 'real' and the objects of belief 'semi-real', which, in modern terms, means that we can know only what *must* be true, and what *could* be false can only be believed. The dictum 'knowledge cannot be mistaken' becomes 'knowledge can only be of what cannot be mistaken', i.e. of indubitable or incorrigible truths. The distinction between knowledge and belief is, therefore, for Plato largely dependent on being able to identify separate objects corresponding to each state of mind.

We should, however, keep open the possibility that, in order to draw an acceptable distinction between knowledge and belief, there may be no need to distinguish between their intrinsic 'objects', that there may be no need to limit the range of propositions which could be known to any special class, for example to necessary truths. We have already noticed that it is customary and, in my view, entirely defensible to assert that the same proposition can be known at one time and believed at another, or known now by me and believed by you. It is not the type of proposition, it can be argued, which distinguishes knowledge and belief; in a situation where someone claims to know something, we do not adjudicate the claim by simple inspection of the proposition and decide on that count alone whether the person knows it or not. We take other considerations into account, for example the reasons or the evidence which the claimant advances to support his claim.

The other main influence, I believe, which has led to the doctrine of infallibility is the widely held conviction that knowledge should be viewed as a system or hierarchy. This implies that there must be foundations which are indubitable or certain or incorrigible. Such a point of view is particularly exemplified by Descartes' attempt to base his system of philosophical knowledge on a basic proposition which was 'indubitable', namely on the certainty of his own existence. The hope was expressed that further certainties could be derived from this basic certainty by rigorous deductive procedures from which the possibility of error was excluded. By this means it was thought that we could achieve a body of knowledge without any weak links. Other philosophers, following a different tradition — that of Hume for example — have regarded propositions about our immediate perceptual experiences, propositions about so-called sense-data, as constituting the basic propositions on which our knowledge of the world must be built. Common to these traditions, which differ so widely in so many respects, is the drawing of a distinction between those items of knowledge which are known independently of inference and those which are known by inference from other items of knowledge. Common, too, is the identification of basic propositions with those which are uninferred, and the crediting of such basic propositions, known non-inferentially either by intuition as in Descartes, or by acquaintance or direct awareness as in the Empiricists, with the characteristic of being 'infallible' or 'incorrigible'. The straightforward distinction between inferred and non-inferred propositions is, of course, acceptable. It could not be the case that all propositions are known as the result of inference since any argument must start from premisses which are themselves, within the context of the argument, uninferred. In everyday life, clearly, many if not most of the things we know come our way without the need for inference.

The acceptance of this distinction does not, however, commit us to the view that there must be some propositions which must in principle be known inferentially, since the same proposition could be known by inference at one time and known without inference at another. Thus, I may have come to know that Drake was buried at sea by inference from a set of premisses: others, such as his contemporaries, may have come to know it 'directly'. Or again, I may have come to know the simple arithmetical proposition '38+37 = 75' by a process of calculation: others may get the answer immediately without recourse to calculation. Nor does it follow, even if there were specific propositions which were in principle uninferred, that they are necessarily incorrigible. Dispensing with inference does not guarantee success: 'basic', in the sense of 'being uninferred' does not confer incorrigibility on a proposition. To those philosophers who view knowledge as a system derived from basic propositions and who insist that knowledge implies infallibility, i.e. that only those propositions can be known which could not be false, this conclusion will give considerable concern. But it will not be of concern to those who hold, as is being held here, that the fact that a proposition could be false does not in itself prevent its being known on occasion by someone.

We are now in a position to consider whether the introduction of the notion of infallibility is required in order to understand our everyday concept of knowledge. I shall try to show that, far from illuminating our everyday concept of knowledge, it distorts it. If it can be shown that it does so, the notion of infallibility should be discarded, unless convincing reasons can be provided to establish that there is some serious deficiency in our everyday concept which can be repaired only by its introduction.

The question may be approached in terms of the distinction

drawn by Professor Ryle in *The Concept of Mind* (London and New York: Hutchinson's University Library, 1949), pp. 149 ff.) between 'achievement words' and 'task words'. Verbs such as 'to win', 'to find', 'to arrive' signify successes of some sort: verbs such as 'to compete', 'to search', 'to travel' signify corresponding task activities. Professor Ryle indicates some of the differences in the logical behaviour of achievement verbs and other verbs of activity or process. Thus achievement verbs signify 'specifiable episodes', while task verbs signify more or less 'protracted proceedings'. Further, whereas it is appropriate to qualify task verbs with adverbs such as 'successfully' or 'unsuccessfully', such qualifications are inappropriately applied to achievement verbs. Thus, competing in a race may be qualified as either successful or unsuccessful, but my winning of a race can be described neither as successful nor as unsuccessful.

There are other features of achievement and task verbs which are relevant to our discussion. From the fact that verbs such as 'to win' or 'to arrive' or 'to find' signify successes, it does not, of course, follow that I am bound to win a race in which I compete, or that travellers have to arrive at their destinations, or that I am bound to find the missing pen for which I am searching. It would be an absurdity to suggest that procedures such as searching, competing and travelling are guaranteed to succeed just because the corresponding achievement verbs cannot signify failures as well as successes. But it would be equally absurd to suggest that achievements, such as winning a race or finding my missing pen or arriving at a destination, are only 'fallible' successes because the corresponding task activities of competing, searching and travelling are subject to failure as well as to success. If I compete in a race and defeat my fellow competitors, my performance of winning is not rendered less meritorious by the fact that there was always the possibility that I might have been defeated. Indeed, there would be no significant meaning to the term 'winning' if it did not entail the possibility of losing. A walk-over is not the paradigm of winning. Nor would it make sense to introduce some notion of winning such that even the possibility of losing was excluded, as some sort of ideal with which 'fallible' winning, i.e. winning where there is the possibility of losing, could be contrasted. If someone were tempted to introduce such a notion, the all-important point is that such a notion would not illuminate our ordinary concept of winning but simply distort it. Similar considerations apply to notions such as finding or discovering. My success in finding something which I have lost is not in any way diminished by the fact that I might have failed to find it. The critical point is that when we are successful in searching for something, i.e. when we find something, it is pointless to depreciate our success by describing it as 'fallible', simply because searching involves the risk of failure. Successes of any sort whatsoever can be qualified neither as 'fallible' nor as 'infallible'.

When we turn to the notion of knowledge, much the same account has, I think, to be given. Although the verb 'to know' signifies a success or achievement, the processes of acquiring knowledge necessarily involve the possibility of error. Learning cannot be in principle fault-free. We must, of course, be careful to distinguish between saying that a person *may* err in the search for knowledge and saying that he *is* in error. We acquire knowledge in a variety of ways, sometimes as the result of lengthy investigations and sometimes quite quickly. We are all slow learners sometimes and quick learners at other times. It took a long time, for example, to discover the chemical composition of penicillin: it would not take any of us very long to find the sum of 687 and 754. Two points need to be stressed here. The first is that whether we discover some item of knowledge slowly or quickly does not in any way affect the status of the knowledge gained. Speed does not confer infallibility. If I try to cross a stream either by jumping across it or by using the stepping stones provided, I equally run the risk of getting my feet wet. If I learn something as the result of a process of inference or, as is very often the case, without resorting to inference, success cannot be guaranteed. The second point is that when we do find the answer to some problem, when we succeed in settling some issue, whenever, that is, we do acquire some item of knowledge, the fact that there was always the risk that we might not have succeeded does not entail any dire consequences. In particular, the fact that we might not have succeeded does not in any way detract from our success when we do succeed, nor does it justify describing our successes as 'fallible'.

I suggest, therefore, that the introduction of some notion of infallible knowledge involving not even the possibility of error, either as a necessary feature of human knowledge itself or as an ideal with which ordinary human knowledge is to be contrasted, is wholly unnecessary. It would, indeed, distort the meaning of the term 'knowledge' just as much as the introduction of a sense of winning, which did not entail the possibility of losing, would distort the sense of winning with which we are familiar. The risk of error in no way rules out the possibility of knowledge, nor does it detract from it when it is achieved. Knowledge is neither fallible nor infallible: achievements just are achievements.

It is not, therefore, plausible to try to rule out ordinary ways of getting knowledge, such as observation or calculation, simply on the grounds that such procedures are susceptible to mistakes: it would have to be shown that they are necessarily doomed to failure. The search for error-free ways of knowing, such as 'intuition' or 'immediate awareness' or 'acquaintance', in order that we can show that knowledge is possible, is unnecessary and fruitless. There are no ways of coming to know which are doomed to perpetual failure any more than there are ways of coming to know which inherently guarantee success. Knowing, as an achievement verb, implies getting something right, but getting something right does not entail 'could not have got it wrong'. It would be as incongruous to say that the things which we can be right about are those things only which we could not be wrong about as it is to say that the only races which we can win are those which we cannot lose.

I conclude, therefore, that the introduction of the notion of infallibility as a requirement of knowledge would serve only to distort the concept of knowledge with which we are familiar. It might be said in reply to this that what is intended by describing human knowledge as 'fallible' is not that it is incomplete so long as there is the possibility of error, but that we can never be completely certain that we have found the answer to some problem, that we can never be certain that some issue has been finally settled. General scepticism of this sort loses a good deal of its appeal when we consider individual knowledge claims made by historians, botanists or chemists, for example, or when we look at some of the certainties of everyday life, such as my knowing that the coal bucket is empty after careful investigation. In any case, the effect of this rejoinder would be merely to deny that knowledge is obtainable at all. It would not be a comment on the nature of knowledge itself but on our inability to achieve it.

It should, however, be made clear that I am far from suggesting that the recognition that 'knowing' is an achievement verb solves all the philosophical problems about knowledge. But I am suggesting that the recognition of this fact has at least the following consequences. It shows that there is no good reason to depart from our common practice of accepting that knowledge claims can justifiably be made in a wide variety of circumstances, at least so far as the logic of the term 'knowledge' is concerned. Certainly, general scepticism that knowledge is unobtainable or that customary ways of getting knowledge are inadmissible because they are 'fallible' should not deter us. In particular, we need not in principle restrict the possibility of knowledge to necessarily true propositions or to self-guaranteeing ways of knowing. Factual, contingently true propositions cannot be ruled out as possible 'objects' of knowledge simply because they could have been false, nor observation ruled out as a possible source of knowledge simply because it is 'subject to error'. So far as 'incorrigible' propositions are concerned, even if we were to conclude that, apart from analytic truths, there are none, this would not mean that knowledge was thereby rendered impossible.

4 The Infallibility Thesis

I have suggested that the Infallibility Thesis—that knowledge must be restricted to situations where the possibility of error is necessarily excluded—is incompatible with our customary use of the verb 'to know' as an 'achievement' or 'success' verb. Nevertheless, this thesis has been widely accepted and has had a pervasive influence affecting many areas of philosophical discussion far beyond the topic of knowledge itself. Since I consider that it has done more harm than almost any other philosophical thesis, I think it is necessary to explore some of its ramifications in greater detail: my hope is that the thesis may be eradicated once and for all if the ways in which it has undermined our understanding of the term 'knowledge' can be clearly exhibited.

One of the implications of the Infallibility Thesis is its restriction of the possibility of knowledge to propositions which in principle cannot be false; a simple inspection of the status of a proposition will, therefore, enable us to determine whether it is something which can be known or merely believed. Thus, if it is a necessarily true proposition, it can be known: if a contingently true proposition, it can only be believed. This is in sharp contrast with some of the assumptions about knowledge which I listed in Chapter 2 as assumptions which I regard as both widespread and justified. The first assumption was that there is, in general, no restriction on the range of topics about which knowledge may be gained. We are prepared in everyday life to consider knowledge claims made in a wide variety of subjects and situations, for example in history, botany, chemistry, etc. as well as in the endless variety of circumstances in daily life where, for example, someone claims to know that it rained in Cardiff yesterday, or that the coal bucket is empty, or that he is looking at a giraffe. In addition, one of the features implicit in our everyday practice is that we do not regard the status of the proposition *per se* as the critical or exclusive factor in determining whether a knowledge claim should be allowed. This applies equally to claims to know the truth of empirical propositions and to necessary truths. Thus, when someone claims to know something we do not simply, or even primarily, inquire what sort of proposition he claims to know and, on finding that it is not a necessary truth automatically rule out any claim which does not involve such a truth; nor, of course, do we automatically allow any claim to know a necessary truth simply because it is a necessary truth. We do not, for instance, dismiss claims made by botanists, lawyers or historians simply on the grounds that the propositions whose truth they claim to know *could* have been false. Nor, indeed, do we concede claims by mathematicians or logicians to know certain mathematical or logical truths simply because the propositions which they advance *could not* be false. We may, of course, dismiss claims made by historians or botanists etc., or by someone in daily life, but there is no one single factor which is always critical in ruling out all knowledge claims. Simple inspection of a proposition will not in itself reveal whether or not it is known by anyone.

In practice, we take a variety of considerations into account when investigating claims to knowledge. Sometimes, indeed, we may pay great regard to the proposition itself; for example, we might well rule out immediately a claim to know that it will snow in London on the first day of 1984, though even here we would not rule it out simply because the proposition is a contingent as opposed to a necessary proposition. On the other hand, we might accept immediately someone's claim to know the truth of a tautology such as 'A book is a book'. Sometimes, again, we pay particular regard to the circumstances in which the claim is made: we might well attach more weight to the claim that the object in the park is a lion, if it is based on observations made in full light as opposed to twilight. At other times we regard the credentials of the claimant as particularly important: we might be more sympathetic to a historical claim made by a Regius Professor than by a schoolboy. And, of course, we pay particular attention to the reasons which the claimant produces in support of his claim.

The second everyday assumption which I listed in Chapter 2 is that we do not expect that knowledge claims in all subject matters should be justified in the same way. We have learned not to judge the pronouncements of lawyers, historians, etc., or the assertions made in everyday life, by the criteria which we apply to the pronouncements of mathematicians and logicians. We do not, for example, charge mathematicians with making careless or prejudiced observations, nor do we charge botanists simply with making slips in calculations when we reject their respective claims. We have come to recognise that there is a radical difference between deducing the necessary consequences of a set of assumptions and asserting that something is true on the basis of evidence. Thus we distinguish between saying what further proposition will be true if a given proposition is true—for example if it is true that I am in Cardiff, then it is true that I am in Wales—and saying, on the basis of observation, that oak trees, unlike cypresses, shed their leaves in the autumn. However, although we make this distinction, we show no inclination in everyday life to restrict the application of knowledge to hypothetical propositions of the 'if ... then' variety, to the exclusion of categorical propositions about what is happening or has happened in the world outside. It would, indeed, be an extraordinarily severe limitation on our use of the term 'knowledge' if we were restricted to saying only that we knew that *if* a given proposition were true, *then* some other proposition would also be true, and forbidden to say that we knew *that* a given proposition was true. Could we, in fact, have learned how to use the word 'know' in expressions such as, 'I know that *if p* is true, *then q* is true', if we could never significantly say 'I know *that p* is in fact true'?

We have, indeed, come to accept that the concern of mathematicians and logicians with abstract principles debars them from giving information about the world in the sense of telling us about the occurrence of this or that event; on the other hand, the concern of historians, botanists, etc. with facts based on observation and experiment prevents them from dealing with purely abstract truths. We do not blame the one for not providing what the other provides. The mathematician and the botanist have different jobs to do, and each has his own criteria of what constitutes success or failure, getting things right or getting things wrong, in his own field. Both are fallible, but for different reasons. The obvious point, which needs to be repeated in the light of what some philosophers say, is that neither the mathematician nor the botanist has the exclusive right to the use of the term 'knowledge'.

Another significant feature in our customary use of the term 'knowledge' needs to be emphasised at this stage. We have seen that the attempt to restrict the possibility of knowledge to such disciplines as mathematics and logic would be inconsistent with everyday practice: it is no less inconsistent to attempt, as many philosophers have done, to extend the range of knowledge beyond logic and mathematics but to restrict it to those situations in everyday life where claims to knowledge *could not* be rejected. Some philosophers, as we have previously noticed, have retreated into incorrigibility by restricting non-mathematical and non-logical claims to knowledge to those pronouncements where there is a presumption that the claimant *cannot* be mistaken, such as 'I know that I've got a headache' (an example of a proposition about my present sensations) or 'It seems to me now as if there were a lion in the park' (an example of a proposition describing my immediate perceptual experience). This retreat is not something dictated to them by our ordinary use of the term 'knowledge' but rather is something which is wholly inconsistent with ordinary usage. We do not automatically allow a claim on someone's part to know that he has a headache and automatically disallow someone's claim to know that the coal bucket is empty when he can see quite clearly that it is empty. Here, again, we can see that inspection of the proposition *per se* will not determine whether or not someone knows that the bucket is empty. Before allowing or dismissing a claim to know that it is empty, we need to know, amongst other things, who is making the claim, whether he knows what a bucket is, whether he knows what it is for something to be empty, and generally the circumstances under which he makes the claim. Why should we think that these conditions *never* could be satisfied?

The crucial point, I think, is to recognise that the concept of knowledge cannot be interpreted in such a way as to give some sort of logical priority to its application in disciplines such as logic and mathematics, so that its application in such disciplines as history and botany, as well as in everyday situations, has to be regarded as somehow degenerate. What cannot be true, either logically or historically, is that we first learned the use of 'to know' in situations of 'incorrigibility' and then extended its use, either through perversity or laxity, to situations where there is the possibility of being mistaken as well as the possibility of being right. To suggest this would be as unplausible as suggesting that we learned to use the concept of 'winning' in walk-over situations and extended it to situations where there was more than one competitor so that races could be lost as well as won. 'Being right' is, of course, part of what is involved in saying that someone knows something. But 'being right', though incompatible with 'actually being wrong', is not restricted in its application to situations where the risk of error is necessarily excluded. 'Being right', in its standard employment rather than in some degenerate sense, means '*is* right, but *could* have been wrong', not '*is* right and *could not* have been wrong'. Getting the right answer to some problem does not presuppose 'could not have got it wrong'.

One of the conditions of introducing the concept of knowledge is that it should be possible to contrast knowledge with what is not knowledge, for example with belief or opinion. To credit someone with believing something is equally to say that he does not know, and *vice versa*, to say that he knows something is to say that he does not just believe it. In a world where there was no contrast between knowledge and opinion, there would be no use for either the term 'knowledge' or the term 'opinion', any more than in a world where the distinction between 'true' and 'false' could not be drawn could there be a use for either term. The normal use of 'knowledge' is, therefore, in situations where we can sometimes say that someone knows something and sometimes that someone merely believes something. Having learned its use in such situations we are able to extend its use to other specialised situations where the contrast between knowledge and opinion is not to be found, for example to mathematics and logic. In such disciplines we do not seem to distinguish between those items which are known and those about which there are only beliefs or opinions, at least to the extent to which we draw this distinction in other disciplines such as history. Geometrical text books, for example, do not distinguish between what is a matter of knowledge and what is only a matter of opinion. This does not, of course, rule out the possibility than on the frontiers of the subject there might be reluctance to claim that certain issues had been settled, nor that an individual may not be in a position to claim knowledge of what is generally regarded as proved. We should regard the use of 'knowledge' in mathematics, for example, as a specialised, rather than the standard, use.

A similar kind of reply must be offered if someone were to suggest that a necessary truth is the paradigm of what a truth should be and that a contingent truth is a truth only in some subordinate sense. We should, indeed, say the reverse. We must start with propositions which can be either true or false and we can extend the use of the term 'true' to specialised situations where propositions can only be necessarily true or necessarily false. Just as it would be absurd to suggest that 'knowledge' should be restricted to those situations where we cannot be mistaken, so it would be absurd to suggest that we should revise our standard practice of allowing that propositions which are only contingently true are properly described as 'true', for example 'Waterloo was fought in 1815', or 'It rained in Cardiff yesterday', etc. Propositions in logic and mathematics, for example, which cannot be false or cannot be true, should be regarded as oddities rather than as the paradigm of what a true or a false proposition should be like. To say that 'true' means 'necessarily true' is absurd. We cannot dismiss non-necessary truths simply because they do not match up to the high standards of necessary truths. We must, therefore, resist the attempt to link the notions of knowledge and necessity in the sense that we can only be right about what could not be false, i.e. that we can know only necessary truths.

The opposition, therefore, between knowledge and belief or opinion is *not* the same as that between, on the one hand, mathematics and logic and, on the other hand, the remaining accredited disciplines together with the assertions made in everyday life. On the contrary, the opposition between knowledge and belief is to be found in every area of mental discipline—in history, botany, politics, etc.—and also, of course, in the assertions of everyday life. Within such disciplines we have learned to distinguish between those issues which may properly be regarded as settled and those which are still in dispute. The fact that sometimes we cannot decide authoritatively whether an issue is settled, say in chemistry or history, or the fact that sometimes we are positively mistaken, does not mean that we never meet with success. Indeed to say of any discipline, such as chemistry, that *everything* within its field is in dispute is, in effect, to deny it the status of a discipline at all. It would be absurd, for example, to regard *everything* in history or chemistry as still disputable and fit matter for research. How could we distinguish what was still disputable if nothing was settled? Precisely the same considerations apply to the assertions we make in everyday life. Though I may well be mistaken in claiming to know that the tower in the far distance is the tower of St John's church, given a little time and a little effort I can hardly be mistaken in claiming to know that the coal bucket under my nose is empty.

The idea that the term 'knowledge' should be reserved for situations where there cannot even be the possibility of error should be seen, therefore, as an attempt on the part of some philosophers to introduce a novel concept of knowledge to supplant the existing one. It cannot be regarded as throwing light on the familiar sense of 'knowledge' but only as a distortion of it. Our ordinary sense of 'knowledge' is geared to situations where mistakes of many sorts are possible, but these are situations where there also exists the possibility of detecting and correcting mistakes. It would have been healthier for the theory of knowledge if philosophers, instead of searching for incorrigible propositions as the only fit 'objects' of knowledge, had busied themselves with studying the methods by which we learn to detect and to correct our mistakes.

The accusations of laxity in our everyday sense of knowledge sometimes made by philosophers are as unfounded as their recommendations that we should replace it by technical senses such as 'apprehension' or 'acquaintance' are unnecessary. The laxity is seen to be there only if we start with the preconception that knowledge should be infallible, a notion which is absent from our everyday practice. It would be wiser to judge philosophers' concepts by the standards of common practice, rather than judge common practice in terms of the requirements of philosophers' theories. I do not wish to suggest that the accusations of laxity are wholly derived from the acceptance of the Infallibility Thesis: as I shall try to elaborate later, they sometimes arise from a failure to see that, very sensibly, we adopt different standards of rigour at different times in conceding claims to knowledge. Thus we do not normally question a claim made by a neighbour or a colleague whom we regard as reliable and scrupulous, based on his own observations, to know so-and-so; the very same claim, however, might be subjected to rigorous examination if it were made by the same person as a witness in a law court. It isn't that we play fast and loose with the word 'know': we adapt our standards of rigour to suit the occasion.

The main reason, however, if my diagnosis is correct, for the rejection of our widespread practice of being prepared to consider and sometimes to concede knowledge claims made in a wide range of topics is the acceptance of the Infallibility Thesis, i.e. the thesis that we can only know what could not in any circumstances be false, as opposed to the modest thesis, which we are all prepared to accept, that when someone knows something, what he knows is true. The rejection of the Infallibility Thesis, as a distortion of our everyday concept of knowledge, frees us from the necessity of abandoning our established practice of giving consideration to the knowledge claims of lawyers, botanists, historians, chemists, etc.

The third assumption which I listed in Chapter 2 as one which we commonly make is that it is both intelligible and justifiable to speak of the same proposition as being known by you and merely believed by me, or being believed by me at one time and known by me at another, for example I might believe that Sir Francis Drake was buried at sea and you might know it. This assumption, again, has been challenged partly on considerations drawn from the Infallibility Thesis and partly because of the view, which is in turn a corollary of the Infallibility Thesis, that knowledge and belief require radically different 'objects', such that an object which is proper to belief can never become an object of knowledge.

The view that knowledge and belief require exclusive objects is to be found in Plato, where it is developed in association with his Theory of Forms. The Theory of Forms, which is the central theme in his Theory of Knowledge, was, no doubt, prompted by a variety of considerations and was intended to solve a variety of problems. Aristotle, however, in two places in the *Metaphysics* (987 a 32 and 1078 b 13) asserts that the primary reason for its introduction was the desire of Plato and his followers to counteract the Heraclitean doctrine that everything which is perceived by the senses is in a state of continual flux, exemplified in the remark 'You cannot step twice into the same river'. Plato thought that it was necessary to resist this Heraclitean doctrine because of an implication which he found quite unacceptable, namely that it would make knowledge impossible. Hence, according to Aristotle, Plato was forced to assert the existence of entities which are permanent and unchanging, independent of the things accessible to the senses, entities which could serve as the objects of knowledge. They would be accessible to 'thought' but not to the senses. Thus Beauty, Truth, Redness, etc. as Forms (or, in the modern idiom, universals) are permanent and unchanging and, therefore, possible objects of knowledge; this beautiful thing, this true statement, this red thing (particulars, in the modern idiom) are subject to change and, therefore, cannot be known. Plato's way of counteracting the sceptical position of the Heracliteans was, therefore, to accept it so far as sense perception goes (i.e. the things which can be sensed are constantly changing and cannot be known), but to reject it for the things accessible only to thought, i.e. the realities which can be thought are permanent and therefore can be known.

Let us, then, see how the argument runs. Clearly, there cannot be a valid inference from the premiss 'Everything which is accessible to the senses is changing' to the conclusion 'Therefore nothing can be known'. Indeed there is no argument here at all. What makes it possible to treat it as an argument is the suppressed premiss 'Nothing which changes can be known'. How, in turn, could this premiss be established? It must itself presuppose the further premiss that knowledge is possible only of what is permanent. How, in turn, is this to be established? Only by means of accepting an arbitrary definition of knowledge as something which is 'infallible', itself based on confusing the truth that what is known is true with 'what is known must be eternally true'. Because of Plato's partiality for talking about the 'objects' of knowledge as entities or things, as opposed to our practice of talking about knowing the *truth of propositions*, 'what is known must be eternally true' becomes for him 'what is known must be unchanging entities', which, in turn, becomes 'what is known must be the "real"'. Rather than reject the suppressed premiss 'Nothing which changes can be known', and thus avoid the conclusion 'Nothing can be known', Plato accepted it because of his identification of what is 'knowable' with what is 'real', i.e. unchanging or permanent. He was thus forced, in order to safeguard the possibility of knowledge, to introduce a duplicated world, the world of Forms or eternal entities, to which the Heraclitean scepticism could not apply.

There is, indeed, no reason why we should accept the curious proposition 'Nothing which changes can be known'. For example, in order to be in a position to assert that something has changed, I must *know* that it has different characteristics now from those it had formerly, i.e. to be able to say that I know that the colour of my hair has changed, I must know that once it was brown and now is grey; and, of course, it is only through sense perception that I can learn that it is different now from what it was. On matters such as these, Reason or Thought (conceived by Plato as the only source of knowledge, where perception can yield only belief) remain silent.

In the *Republic* (476 ff.) Plato tries to establish two positions which are relevant to our discussion, namely that knowledge and belief require different 'objects' and that the objects of belief cannot be 'real'. We shall follow his arguments. The argument for the first position is as follows. Plato starts by defining knowledge and belief as 'faculties' or 'powers', and adds that faculties can be distinguished only by their different functions and their different objects. Just as sight and hearing are faculties which are distinguished by what they do and what they are directed to, since they have neither colour nor shape nor any of the similar qualities which enable us to distinguish other things one from another, so knowing and believing are to be distinguished by the fact that the function of knowledge is 'knowing' and its object 'the real' and the function of belief is 'believing' and its object 'the semi-real'. The comparison between knowing and believing on the one hand and sight and hearing on the other is particularly unfortunate. In one sense, it is true to say that the 'objects' of sight and hearing are different: the one is concerned with 'sights' and the other with 'sounds', which are, of course, different. But in another sense of 'object', it is plainly absurd to say that the 'objects' of sight and hearing are different, i.e. whereas it is true that I cannot hear smells or sights nor see sounds, I can both see and hear an aeroplane or a bell, and in this sense of 'object', it is absurd to say that 'each faculty has its own objects'. Plato seems to have been misled by the ambiguity in the term 'object' as either (a) a sort of internal accusative, e.g. where we can say that the object of seeing is sights or the object of knowledge is 'knowings' or (b) as a thing or entity, e.g. where we can say that one of the things which I can see is an aeroplane or one of the things which I can hit is a nail.

There is a further respect in which the comparison with seeing is unfortunate, namely the suggestion that knowing, like seeing, is some sort of *act* or *activity* which can be directed upon an object in the sense of an entity. The familiar sense of 'knowledge' is that in which we say that what we know are propositions, expressed in the form 'I know *that* Great Britain is an island', where there is neither the suggestion that knowing is a specific act which I perform at a particular time, nor the suggestion that there is some sort of confrontation between the mind and some object or entity. Many philosophers, as we shall see later, have accepted Plato's view that in addition to propositional knowledge there is also the sense of knowledge in which it is to be regarded as a specific act or confrontation with a thing, for example 'intuiting a truth', 'being acquainted with a sense-datum or a feeling', 'apprehending a fact', etc. Indeed, they have usually regarded this sense as exhibiting what knowledge is *par excellence*.

The argument that different faculties must have different objects is, indeed, unconvincing when applied to intellectual faculties. Do we need to distinguish separate objects for every different faculty? Asserting, for instance, is different from assuming, and imagining is different from perceiving; but there is no reason why you cannot assume what I assert, or I imagine what you perceive. Further, from the fact that asserting and assuming may be concerned with the same objects, it does not in the least follow that we must therefore identify assuming with asserting, any more than from the fact that I can both pass and kick a rugby ball it follows that kicking and passing have to be identified. Similarly, the fact that knowing is different from believing does not entail that their objects, in the sense of *what* is known and *what* is believed, must be different; and the fact that knowing and believing can be directed to the same objects, i.e. propositions, does not entail that knowing and believing must be identified. Plato, I think rightly, wished to assert that there was a fundamental difference between knowledge and belief, but wrongly assumed that they could be differentiated only if it could be shown that they were concerned with radically different objects.

The arguments by means of which Plato tries to establish that the objects of belief, unlike those of knowledge, cannot be 'real' are no more felicitous. The proposition that everything which is sensible is changing is interpreted by Plato thus: particular sensible objects, such as 'this beautiful thing', 'this large thing', 'this heavy thing', have contradictory characteristics inasmuch as something which appears beautiful to me may appear ugly to you; something which is heavy from one point of view may appear light from another point of view, etc. The conclusion is then drawn that nothing which has contradictory characteristics can be 'fully real': particular sensible things must be placed in a limbo between existence and non-existence. The superficial plausibility of this argument depends, of course, on treating expressions such as 'being beautiful', 'being light', 'being heavy' as if they represented qualities which something could possess: it would, indeed, be

same time. But the initial plausibility vanishes when we distinguish between saying that something has a particular quality and
saying that something stands in a certain relation to something
else. There is, of course, nothing contradictory in one thing, X,
standing in one relation, such as 'being taller than', to another
thing, Y, and standing in another relation, such as 'being shorter
than', to another thing Z. A contradiction would arise only if the
same thing, X, stood in opposite relations to the same thing, Y, for
example if I were both taller than and shorter than John at the
same time.

One of the general conclusions which Plato draws from arguments such as these is that the objects of belief, which he identifies
with 'sensible things' have an existence inferior to that of the
objects of knowledge. From this it follows that perception, identified by Plato with the sphere of belief, must be discarded as a
possible source of knowledge. This is the genesis of the fatal
dichotomy between 'thought' and 'perception' as rival sources of
knowledge, the influence of which is with us still. Hence the view
that necessary truths, accessible to 'thought' unadulterated by
perception, are the only things which can be known. The whole
edifice is built on the foundation of the Infallibility Thesis, and
collapses with the collapse of the thesis.

Before considering in more detail subsequent attempts to discredit perception as a source of knowledge, we should notice a
contemporary version of the doctrine that knowledge and belief
must have separate objects. Some philosophers, wishing like Plato
to distinguish radically between knowledge and belief, but being
unwilling to accept the Platonic distinction between Forms or
Universals as the objects of knowledge and particulars as the
objects of belief, have drawn a distinction between 'facts' as the
objects of knowledge and 'propositions' as the objects of belief.
Knowledge is conceived as an unique intellectual activity
superior to the 'inferior' attitudes of belief, opinion, assumption,
etc. The latter are said to be concerned with propositions which
can be either true or false: knowledge is some kind of direct
confrontation with a 'fact', conceived of as a different entity from a
proposition and given a special status as an existent. There is,
however, no need and no warrant for the introduction of 'facts' as
entities different from propositions to serve as the exclusive
objects of knowledge. The view that they are required is just

another version of the Infallibility Thesis: all that is needed is that we should distinguish between knowledge and belief in terms of saying that what we believe, assume, etc. may be either true or false propositions, whereas what we know can only be a true proposition. (I am here disregarding the use of 'know' where the verb 'to know' is followed by nouns, for example where we speak of knowing places, such as Blackpool, or persons, such as Churchill: 'facts', in the relevant sense, are regarded as entities quite different from places or people). Just as we resisted earlier the conclusion, prompted by the Infallibility Thesis, that we can know only what *cannot* be false, so we must now resist the conclusion that knowledge requires 'facts' as separate entities from propositions, merely to satisfy the requirement that what is known is true while what is believed may be true or false. 'Facts' are just true propositions. Since the equation of 'fact' with 'false proposition' is disallowed, there cannot be 'false facts'. Indeed, 'facts' can be described neither as 'true' nor as 'false': not as 'true' since this would be otiose, nor as 'false', since, as true propositions, this would be self-contradictory.

There is, then, no need to depart from our established practice of assuming that different cognitive attitudes can be directed to the same 'object', i.e. proposition. I may believe what you know to be true, for example that Madagascar is an island; you may assume to be true what I assert to be true, etc. If we are to introduce separate objects for belief and knowledge, arguments must be produced other than those based on the acceptance of the Infallibility Thesis. The fact that the thesis involves such an unplausible move, which represents such a departure from ordinary practice, is itself an argument against its acceptance.

In conclusion, it must be emphasised that the rejection of separate objects for knowledge and belief does not in itself warrant the conclusion that there is no radical difference between knowledge and belief: it certainly does not in itself warrant the view that knowledge is a species of belief or that knowledge can be defined in terms of belief. Even though they may 'share the same objects' in the sense that what we know and what we believe equally are propositions, there may well be differences between them so great as to prohibit the defining of one in terms of the other. However, before we consider this problem, we must first examine the influence of the Infallibility Thesis in another direction, namely on the status of perception and its claim to be a possible source of knowledge.

5 Knowledge and Perception

The Infallibility Thesis and the related thesis of separate objects for knowledge and belief can be seen from the earliest times (e.g. in Plato) as the chief reason for the prolonged attack on perception and the attempt to discredit it as a possible source of knowledge. We have already seen how Plato attempted to relegate perception to the sphere of belief on the grounds that the things which are accessible to the senses are subject to constant change, and so cannot be known. From Plato to the present day, succeeding philosophers of many persuasions have, on various grounds, rejected the claims of perception to provide knowledge. Descartes, an example of a so-called 'rationalist' philosopher, found three reasons for dismissing perception, namely (a) that the senses must be regarded as unreliable because they have 'deceived' us on many occasions, (b) since there is no fixed criterion by means of which we can authoritatively decide when we are awake and when we are asleep, it may well be that everything which we claim to know is in fact false, and (c) for all we know, we may be the creatures of a malignant demon who takes pleasure in allowing us to be mistaken about everything. Further, contemporary philosophers, particularly so-called 'empiricists', have taken over Descartes's first reason for rejecting perception as a source of knowledge and, with suitable modifications, converted it into the formidable 'Argument from Illusion'.

A common feature of the many versions of this argument is the attempt to show that there are occasions when we are 'deceived by our senses', for example a stick which normally appears straight looks bent when it is seen immersed in water; objects which look circular from one angle may look elliptical from another; people suffering from *delirium tremens* 'see' pink rats; people in the desert sometimes see mirages; sometimes I mistake the bush in my garden for a lion, etc. Three different conclusions have been drawn from such considerations:

1. The general sceptical conclusion is sometimes drawn that if the senses are untrustworthy on particular occasions, they must be regarded as untrustworthy as a whole, since we have no means of telling when the information which they give is 'veridical' and when it is not. The argument seems to be based on the principle: if sometimes wrong, then perhaps always wrong. Perception is precluded from ever providing knowledge because of the failings of particular examples of perception.

2. The particular sceptical conclusion is drawn that we can never 'really' be certain of any individual perceptual claim. The reason for this is that the establishment of any claim would involve an endless series of verification procedures and since we cannot, in fact, complete an endless series of tests, the most that we could achieve is probability. To establish the truth of the proposition 'The bucket is empty' would, it is alleged, involve an endless series of tests, which precludes the possibility of complete verification.

3. The third conclusion is concerned not so much with the trustworthiness or otherwise of perception as with the 'objects' of perception, i.e. with determining what it is we 'actually' or 'directly' see, hear, taste, etc. The Argument from Illusion is regarded by its exponents as demonstrating that the plain man's alleged claim to see *things*, such as books, mountains, castles, etc. (often referred to by philosophers as 'material' or 'physical' objects) must be, at least in part, withdrawn. The fact that mistakes occur, so it is argued, shows that sometimes, at least, we do not see things as they 'really' are, or sometimes we do not see what we think we see, such as books, castles, etc., but only the 'appearances' of things, so-called 'sense-data', usually expressed in terms of shapes, sounds, colours, etc. as opposed to *things*. Hence we have the Sense-Datum Theory of Perception, often allied to the Argument from Illusion, as an attempted answer to the question of what we 'actually' see in perception. There is, however, no uniform account of what sense-data are: sometimes they are described as 'parts of the surfaces of things', sometimes as entities quite different from things: sometimes as private, mental entities, sometimes as neutral, public entities. Some exponents of

the theory have been content to assert that *sometimes* what we perceive are sense-data rather than things: others have claimed that we *never* perceive things but always only sense-data, such as colours, shapes, etc. Others, unable to resist the remorseless logic of the argument, have concluded that there *are* no things: there are only sense-data.

The scope of this essay precludes a discussion of the Sense-Datum Theory in general, but there is one important feature of the theory which directly concerns us, namely the attempt, sometimes implicit in the theory and sometimes explicit, to rehabilitate perception as a form or source of knowledge. This feature, indeed, is regarded by some of its defenders as perhaps its greatest virtue. The claim of the Sense-datum theorists comes to this. If we describe what we actually perceive in terms of seeing physical or material objects, books, castles, etc., we transcend what is actually 'given' in sensation, and there is always the possibility of error. On the other hand, by substituting sense-data as the things which we 'directly' perceive for material objects which are only 'indirectly' perceived, we eliminate the risk of error. Or, as it is sometimes expressed, if we restrict our perceptual reports to what is 'immediately given' in sensation, such reports will be 'incorrigible'. 'I am looking at a tomato' is corrigible: 'I am having reddish, bulgy sense-data' is incorrigible. The interesting feature is that, whereas the initial force of the Argument from Illusion was to discredit perception as a possible source of knowledge, the effect of the Sense-Datum Theory is to rehabilitate perception as a form of knowledge, provided that perceptual reports are expressed in the sense-datum terminology. To what extent are these three conclusions acceptable?

1. The reply to the first conclusion, namely that perception must be regarded as untrustworthy as a whole because individual perceptions are untrustworthy, is the familiar reply that a general sceptical argument such as this is self-defeating. We can only show that the senses have deceived us in a particular case by accepting that other perceptions are reliable, for example I can only conclude that I am mistaken in thinking that I can see a lion in the garden by accepting that what I am seeing is a bush. We could only have introduced the notion of being mistaken about what we see, hear, etc. if we could presuppose the possibility of being able to confirm other perceptions. Procedures of falsification are possible only if there are procedures of confirmation at

hand. There are, it seems to me, three absurdities which are involved here:

(a) It makes sense, of course, to question an individual perceptual report, such as my report that I can see a lion in the garden, in a variety of circumstances and for a variety of reasons, for instance if made in unfavourable light conditions, or because of the inherent improbability of such an event. No one would claim that statements made on the basis of observation are *never* mistaken: the insinuation, on the part of some philosophers, that this represents the view of the 'plain man' is without foundation. But it makes no sense to reject perception *per se*, or to reject it in general because of occasional mistakes.

(b) It is absurd to introduce into any sphere the possibility of committing mistakes without also recognising the ability to correct them. If we can detect mistakes, we must also, in principle, be able to correct them. The impression that, so far as perception goes, we are in a state of utter helplessness, bewildered by our inability to detect when we are wrong and therefore incapable of knowing when we are right, is just a piece of philosophical naïvety. I can, of course, make mistakes in mathematical calculations, but this would not be considered an adequate reason for rejecting mathematical calculations in general. Sometimes I can detect my own mistakes, and sometimes other people detect them for me; sometimes I can correct them myself by further, perhaps more careful, calculations and sometimes I rely on the calculations of others, more expert than I. So it is with perception. If I make a mistake myself—if I mistake one thing for another, say a bush for a lion, a Rolls for a Bentley, vodka for sulphuric acid—I can correct my mistake by further, perhaps more careful or more prolonged observations, or I can accept correction from others, better positioned or more expert than myself. I can summon my ears to help my eyes, and there are usually plenty of gadgets around, such as measuring rods, telescopes, litmus paper, etc. which I can make use of. What sort of people would we be if we could detect mistakes but never correct them? If, for example, we could tell when a key did not fit a lock, but were constitutionally incapable of telling when we had found the right key? We can here, I think, detect the Infallibility Thesis lurking in the background admonishing us that, if perception is not 'incorrigible' in the sense that it can never be wrong, we should put no trust in it. We can know, it warns, only where we can't be wrong; we can win only where we can't lose.

(c) The third absurdity lies in the notion that there is some higher court, such as Reason or Logic, which sits in judgement on perception and rules out its claim, in certain circumstances, to provide knowledge. As we have seen, 'mistakes' in perception can be detected only by other perceptions, and they can be corrected only by further perceptions. Critics of perception seem to have persistently disregarded this self-correcting aspect of perception. It would, of course, be a travesty of the truth to represent the apparent opposition between the claim that the sun is roughly the size of a football and the claim that the sun is so many million miles in diameter, as an opposition between the incorrect deliverance of Perception and the correct deliverance of Reason respectively. The deliverances of Reason and Logic with regard to perception, if there were any, would be to the effect that we should not reject what we know to be true: that we know, for example in certain circumstances that the coal bucket is empty, or that the object in the garden is a bush and not a lion.

2. The reply to the second conclusion, namely that we can never be 'really' certain of any individual perceptual claim is threefold.

(a) In the first place, its plausibility depends on giving a particular interpretation to the notion of 'proof', that is, demonstration or deductive proof, such as is practised in logic and mathematics, and then imposing this interpretation on all situations where we can be said to confirm something. If, then, procedures of confirmation, apart from mathematical or logical demonstration, involve even the theoretical possibility of error, their claims to provide knowledge must be discarded on general grounds. But confirming the truth of some factual matter is simply different from deducing the consequences of an assumption. Why should historians and chemists, for instance, be required to adopt the same interpretation of 'proof' as mathematicians if their conclusions and their procedures are quite different? The types of mistake which occur in factual investigations are different from those that can occur in mathematical calculations, and, likewise, the methods of detecting errors and eradicating them differ. The habit of some earlier philosophers of drawing a sharp contrast between deduction as the only form of 'necessary reasoning' and induction as a form of 'probable reasoning' no doubt contributed greatly to this distortion of the relationship between mathematical and non-mathematical disciplines. This was particularly apparent in those philosophers who grouped together all non-mathematical or non-logical procedures as 'inductive', as if there were some one simple procedure which they all shared. The distortion is further increased when induction itself is described in grossly over-simple terms as the patient piling up of positive instances, a task which can never be completed and which is always liable to be made fruitless by the appearance of just one negative instance. Not only is it mistaken to think that historians and chemists have the same sorts of problems and the same single method of trying to solve them; the picture of the chemist as one, like Tantalus, reaching for the delicious fruits of certainty which he can never grasp is grotesque. How many times must a chemist analyse common salt before he can justifiably claim to know that it is a compound of the metal sodium and the gas chlorine? It is not surprising, therefore, that those philosophers who made the simple contrast between deduction and induction and who re-garded induction as inevitably hazardous, should have attempted the impossible and unnecessary task of trying to convert induction into deduction. What is needed, instead, is a study of the many types of procedures which are used in the wide range of non-logical and non-mathematical disciplines, paying particular at-tention to the methods by means of which mistakes are detected and eradicated.

(b) The second reply to the doctrine that no particular per-ceptual claim can be conclusively justified is as follows. Not only does the doctrine involve the absurdity of introducing alien standards into non-mathematical disciplines, i.e. judging history or chemistry by the standards appropriate to mathematics; it makes nonsense of the notion of introducing standards at all. It represents an attempt to impose on other accredited methods of proof, such as are available in history or chemistry, standards which are impossibly high, or, indeed, necessarily unattainable.

There cannot, of course, be a simple logical formula by the application of which we could always determine with certainty when the reasons offered to substantiate a given conclusion are 'adequate', or when the evidence produced is 'enough': nor would a student of inductive logic hanker after such a formula. There is no simple way of determining how many tests I must make before concluding justifiably that the bush in my garden is a bush and not a lion: there is no single formula by means of which historians can decide with certainty when the evidence for 1815 as the date of the Battle of Waterloo is enough or botanists decide how many observations are required before they can justifiably claim that oak trees shed their leaves in this country in the autumn. The absence of such a formula does not in practice prevent us from drawing a distinction between 'enough' and 'not enough' evidence in particular cases. Nor does the fact that in particular situations we are sometimes, or even often, uncertain whether we should accept a knowledge claim based on perception deter us at other times from accepting some claims and rejecting others.

The point of introducing standards is that they should be things which we *can* operate, not things which we *could not*. Thus, standards which are immune from even the possibility of theoretical doubt, which set their sights so high that, in principle, they could never be satisfied, are no standards at all. The attempt to satisfy the demand that the notions of 'enough evidence' or 'adequate reasons' should have precisely the same logical status as 'satisfying rigorous deductive rules', would involve the introduction of such necessarily unattainable standards. The scientist in the laboratory will impose rigorous, non-deductive standards upon himself and his associates; the historian in collecting and studying his material will impose his own high standards. They are the best judges of their own successes and their failures. The onlooker or the amateur is in no position to tell at a glance at what point a historian has amassed enough evidence to make a knowledge claim, or at what stage the chemist in repeating his experiments could justifiably call it a day.

(c) Our third reply to the doctrine that individual perceptual statements can never be certain, since we could never complete an endless series of verification procedures, is the point, so forcibly made by J. L. Austin in *Sense and Sensibilia* (Oxford: The Clarendon Press, 1962, p. 118) that it is based on the misconception that all 'statements about "material things" *as such* need to be verified'. The doctrine wrongly suggests that we are always uncertain of the truth of the statements we make, based on our observations, until we have verified them, or at least that a process of verification would add to our confidence in their truth. But the position is, as Austin points out, that there are any number of assertions which we regularly make which need no verification at all. For example, if I look inside the coal bucket, rummage around with my hands and announce that the coal bucket is empty, I, at least need no process of verification to add to my certainty; you, on the other hand, having filled the bucket only recently, may need to verify my assertion before you accept it. For me, knowing on the basis of my observations that the bucket is empty, nothing could count as verifying that the bucket was empty. As Austin remarks (p. 118) one of the sources of this error is 'neglecting *the circumstances in which* things are said', or, in my terms, thinking that it is the status of the proposition *per se* which determines whether it can be known or not by anybody.

I have now considered and rejected the two main arguments which have been advanced to try to show that perception cannot provide knowledge, namely the general argument that perception as a whole is untrustworthy because of the failings of some individual perceptions, and the particular argument that we can never be certain of the truth of any individual perceptual report. There remains to be considered the attempt, based on the Sense-Datum Theory of Perception, to rehabilitate perception as a form of knowing by contending that perceptual reports, if expressed in the sense-datum terminology, can be 'incorrigible'. Consideration of this must, however, be delayed until the relation between perception and knowledge has been more closely examined.

We may approach the question in the following way. Philosophers often speak as if it were the case that whenever I report what I have observed, I am making a knowledge claim. Even further from the truth is the suggestion or assumption sometimes made that, whenever I report what I have seen or heard, I am claiming that my report is 'incorrigible'. Of course, one instance of falsifying a perceptual report would suffice to discredit this supposed identification of perception and knowledge. If I am asked what I observed on my way to College, I do not normally reply 'I know that I saw an elephant in the High Street'. I merely say 'I saw an elephant in the High Street'. Indeed, the occasions for such expressions as 'I know I saw an elephant in the High Street' are relatively rare—limited, indeed, to those occasions when my normal form of reply, 'I saw an elephant', in reply to your question, 'What did you see?' is questioned. Normally we do not query someone's statements about what he sees, hears, etc. But if there is something in the situation which makes us suspicious, we may raise doubts. The speaker's insistence that 'he knows' is in response to such doubts, and is not the normal statement of what he sees, hears, etc. Indeed, it would make no sense to accost someone and open a conversation with 'I know I saw an elephant this morning'. Nor could such a form of address be defended on the grounds that it is merely redundant though quite significant, since we are to assume that whenever anyone says 'I saw an elephant', what he really means is 'I know that I saw an elephant', i.e. as if every time we reported what we saw we were covertly making a knowledge claim. The function of 'I know' in such expressions is merely one of emphasis: it is equivalent to 'I *did* see an elephant'. Except as an emphatic way of re-stating 'I saw an elephant', expressions of the form 'I know I saw . . . ' are without significance. I am not saying merely that we do not as a matter of fact use expressions such as 'I know I saw . . . ' as an opening remark, but that if someone were to speak thus, we would be at a loss to understand him.

We should contrast with this the situation where someone asks 'Do you know where the lion is?', and you reply 'Yes, it's in the garden' (perhaps with the addition 'I know it is'). This elicits the further question 'Why do you say, or what makes you say that it is in the garden?', to which you reply 'Because I saw it there a few moments ago, eating the rhubarb.' Clearly the observation report, 'I saw it . . .', is not itself a knowledge claim, but is introduced to justify a claim to know where the lion is. 'Seeing' is no more 'knowing' than it is 'believing': observation reports must not be construed as reporting acts or processes of knowing nor as covertly implying the making of irrefutable knowledge claims. At the same time, it is true that I may well invoke observation reports, either my own or someone else's, to justify my claim to know that the lion is in the garden, etc.

The fundamental mistake, therefore, which has been committed by many of the critics and supporters of perception alike, is the mistake of assimilating perception to knowledge, of treating perceiving as if it were a *form* or a *way* of knowing. This mistake has been made at two levels. Perceiving has frequently been identified with sensing, i.e. with seeing, hearing, tasting, etc., and sensing has been identified with knowing. But neither seeing nor hearing nor tasting is a way of knowing: smelling a rose is not to be identified with 'knowing a rose', though, of course, in order to know that what I am smelling is a rose, a good deal of knowledge has to be presupposed. Smelling, in itself, can be described neither as correct nor as incorrect; it is not an intellectual activity. As Austin remarks (*op. cit.*, p. 11), 'our senses are dumb . . . our senses do not *tell* us anything, true or false'. Other philosophers have regarded perceiving as a combination of sensing and thought, so that in place of 'seeing' we can now speak of 'observing'. But even at this level it is mistaken to assimilate perceiving to knowing. The mere fact that observing can be either correct or incorrect shows that the straight identification of observing with knowing (which cannot be) is impossible. But the basic reason why the assimilation is misplaced is that knowing, unlike observing, is not something which we *do*. Whereas 'observing the lion in the garden' is a possible activity, 'knowing that the lion is in the garden' is no sort of activity. It is not an act which we perform at a particular time. Thus, you don't stop knowing that the lion is in the garden when you stop looking at it. To say, therefore, that someone knows that the lion is in the garden is not to say that he is doing anything, though it may mean that, in order to have found this out, he may well have done many things, such as observing.

The assimilation of perceiving to knowing is not the only false assimilation which some philosophers have made. It is equally mistaken to regard 'inferring' or 'reasoning' or 'deducing' or 'calculating' as if they were 'forms of knowing'. Knowing is not, in itself, something which we *do*; knowledge is something we get by doing things such as observing, calculating or inferring. Thus, to say of a scientist that he knows that the earth revolves round the sun is not to say what he is doing either now or at any time, though to say that he knows implies that he *has* done many things, for example made observations, calculations, etc. We must distinguish between the means of getting knowledge and knowledge itself. The defence of this position will be one of the themes of the next chapter.

Often, as I have suggested, when someone reports what he has seen etc. we accept what he says without asking for reasons or evidence. This is not to say that we agree that he has said something which is incorrigible, something which in no circumstances could be false, but merely that he has said something which we did not wish to question because, for example, we knew he was right. It does not, of course, follow that because some reports are accepted without question on a particular occasion that they will be accepted without question on all occasions; my report that I saw a lion in the garden might be accepted by you in casual conversation, but questioned in a law court. If, then, when I report what I have seen there is no presumption that I am claiming that I am knowing something, and far less that I am claiming to know something 'infallibly', the contention which is the basis of the Argument from Illusion that my reports are sometimes incorrect has little force, and the further contention that perhaps we never know when they are correct has even less force.

It is not, therefore, surprising that some philosophers, such as Plato and Descartes, starting with the twin assumptions that perception *should* be a form of knowledge and that knowledge is necessarily 'infallible' or 'incorrigible', have despaired of perception once they have realised that 'mistakes' can enter into perceptual reports, or that the senses sometimes 'deceive' us. It was inevitable that they should relegate perception to the inferior realm of belief. Knowledge, for such philosophers, can be found only in the sphere of Reason, operating predominantly in such fields as mathematics and logic, or in those fields where intuition can take over from perception. In this respect, empirically minded philosophers have joined forces with their 'rationalist' counterparts in rejecting the aspirations of perception to provide knowledge, as can be seen in such assertions as 'the notion of certainty does not apply to empirical knowledge' and 'no empirical propositions can be more than probable', assertions which have been widely made in this century. Attempts on both fronts to discredit perception are traceable, I have tried to show, to the combination of defining knowledge in terms of infallibility and assimilating perceiving to knowing. Historians of philosophy who see a total opposition between the rival 'schools' of 'rationalists' and 'empiricists' should note this common feature. They should also note that the widely held view that empirical knowledge can never be certain is equally indebted to the disastrous identification by Plato of knowledge with infallibility and the disastrous identification by Hume of knowledge with 'the having of impressions', i.e. with perception.

Not all philosophers, of course, have been able to accept the simple picture that knowledge is obtainable only of necessary truths and that all contingent propositions can only be believed. Even some empirically minded philosophers have fought shy of this conclusion. But even in their case, the influence of the Infallibility Thesis is apparent. Wishing to salvage some knowledge outside the fields of logic and mathematics, but retaining the thesis that knowledge must be incorrigible, they have turned to 'immediate experiences' as a possible source of knowledge. This move has resulted in the rehabilitation of perception as a source or form of knowledge, but at a considerable price.

3. We are now able to reply to the third conclusion which some philosophers have drawn from such arguments as the Argument from Illusion. This conclusion was to the effect that, by substituting 'sense-data' for 'material objects' as the immediate objects of perception, we could achieve incorrigibility. Alternative versions of the same theme are that we should substitute the 'sense-datum terminology' for the 'material object terminology', or that we should confine ourselves to such expressions as 'It seems to me now as if there were a lion in the garden' in place of 'There's a lion in the garden'. To this we must reply as follows:

(a) There were, no doubt, many reasons for the introduction of the Sense-Datum Theory in one or other of its forms. If, however, one of the reasons for its introduction (I think the basic reason) was that by saying such things as 'I am having lionish sense-data' or 'It seems to me as if there were a lion . . .' instead of 'There's a lion . . .' we could acquire incorrigible propositions so that knowledge would be possible, then such substitutions are wholly unnecessary. There is no need to hunt for incorrigible propositions in order to make knowledge possible, since the possibility of acquiring knowledge in any sphere does not depend either on there being incorrigible propositions or on foolproof methods of discovery. The fact that the proposition 'The coal bucket is empty' is a contingent and not an incorrigible proposition does not in itself automatically prevent me from knowing that it is true in any possible circumstance. This is just another example of the familiar doctrine based on the mistaken premises that knowledge must be infallible, i.e. confined to propositions which *could* not be false, and that perception, or at least some element in perception, such as sensing, 'ought' to be knowledge. When, therefore, we realise that perceptual reports are sometimes mistaken, the appropriate action to be taken is to emphasise that there are ways and means of detecting and correcting such mistakes, rather than to try to cut down perception to the size when it will fit the 'infallibility' mould. As Professor Ryle remarked in *The Concept of Mind* (London and New York: Hutchinson's University Library, 1949, p. 238), what we need is 'not inoculation against mistakes, but ordinary precautions against them, ordinary tests for them and ordinary corrections of them'. This point can be generalised. All sorts of human activities can be described as either correctly or incorrectly done. We can observe correctly or incorrectly; we can make invalid as well as valid inferences; we can make mistakes in calculations as well as getting them right. But we do not assume that no observations can be correct because some are admittedly incorrect, that no inferences can be valid because some are admittedly invalid, and that we can never get our sums right because we sometimes get them wrong. The mere fact that an activity can be correctly or incorrectly done does not mean that success is impossible, nor should it tempt us to try to devise foolproof methods of observing, inferring, calculating, etc.

(b) In the second place, we must question the attempt to locate 'incorrigible' propositions in the realm of matters of fact to match the 'necessarily true' propositions of logic and mathematics. If by an 'incorrigible' proposition is meant a proposition which in no circumstances could be false, then it is hard to see how a contingent proposition such as 'I am having lionish sense-data' or 'It seems to me as if there were a lion . . .' could be incorrigible. As many writers have pointed out, I could be mistaken not only in the sense that I have misdescribed what I see in the sense of applying the wrong words, but also misdescribed what I see in the sense of making a positive mistake, for example not just made a verbal slip and called a rhinoceros an elephant but actually taken a rhinoceros to be an elephant. Nor, of course, could we avoid the possibility of mistake by switching from nouns to adjectives, i.e. from talking about elephants to talking about 'elephantine sense-data'.

If, on the other hand, by 'incorrigible' is meant that it would be absurd in practice to question some propositions, taking into account the circumstances in which they are put forward, as opposed to 'cannot in principle be questioned', then we may allow with equanimity that propositions may be incorrigible. But there is no need whatsoever to restrict such propositions to those expressed in the sense-datum terminology. As Austin points out (*op. cit.*, p. 114), the proposition 'That's a pig', uttered in suitable circumstances, would be incorrigible in the sense that nothing could be produced which would show that the speaker had made a mistake. We see here again an example of the mistake of assuming that it is the nature of the proposition itself which makes it 'knowable' or 'believable'. The same proposition, 'That's a pig', could be incorrigible if uttered in the circumstances described by Austin, and corrigible if uttered in other situations, for example where the speaker took little care or was very hazy about what pigs look like, etc. Thus, what makes a particular proposition appear incorrigible is not its own nature as a proposition, but the circumstances under which it is made. We must not be misled by the fact that many propositions, when they have become 'common knowledge', find their way into reference books or text books as propositions which are 'known' (e.g. the date of the Battle of Hastings or the atomic weight of tin) into thinking that being 'known' or being 'knowable' is the prerogative of a proposition in itself. In favourable circumstances, therefore, where, for instance, I examine the bucket with care, rummage around inside, turn it upside down, etc., I can declare that the coal bucket is empty as an incorrigible proposition, since nothing could count as falsifying it and no further tests would add in any way to its credentials. However, since, as I have tried to show, the possibility of acquiring knowledge does not depend on a proposition being incorrigible, it does not much matter whether we decide to describe such propositions as 'The coal bucket is empty', as incorrigible or not. What we must do is avoid the twin errors of thinking that a proposition cannot be known unless it is incorrigible, and thinking that incorrigibility is an inherent property of a proposition.

(c) The argument for introducing the Sense-Datum Theory is sometimes put in the form that by substituting sense-data for material objects, or by substituting the sense-datum terminology for the material object terminology, we are able to provide an unvarnished report of what is 'given' to us in sensation. Such reports, it is claimed, as the reports of what is 'actually given', cannot but be accurate and must be accepted as items of knowledge. They are then contrasted with the reports given by perception in the material object language, where, it is claimed, there is always the possibility of error since such reports involve interpretation on our part and, since they involve a jump beyond what is given, must be in principle hazardous. Thus, if I confine myself to what is given, for example 'I am having red, bulgy sense-data', I cannot be wrong; if I say 'I can see a tomato', using my past experience, I may well be mistaken. But this contrast between two reports, the one unvarnished and 'given' and the other interpreted, is fictitious. It is fictitious for two main reasons: (1) sensation does not issue any reports. The senses in themselves—tasting, touching, etc.—say nothing. Sensation, as we have noticed earlier, is not a way of knowing. (2) In the required sense of 'given', nothing is given in sensation. When I open my eyes and look at something, nothing is given in the sense that all I have to do is accept, without any kind of interpretation, what is offered. Nothing in the world is labelled except where we have put our labels. In order to be able to say 'I am having bulgy, tomatoish data', I must already know what it is for something to look like a tomato. I must recognise or be able to identify 'what I sense', and to do this I must have acquired the relevant concepts. There is always the possibility of mis-identification, of the misuse of concepts. This is to say that the notion of the 'given' is grossly misleading and hence that the notion of unvarnished, uninter-preted reports, whose accuracy is guaranteed, must be discarded. There is just one report, which may or may not be mistaken, namely 'There's a tomato'.

I conclude, therefore, that both the attempt to rule out per-ception *in toto* as a possible source of knowledge and the attempt to salvage something from perception in the form of incorrigible propositions 'given' in sensation have to be rejected.

The other sphere in which some philosophers claim to have located incorrigible propositions is that of propositions which describe my present feelings, for example 'I am in pain', 'I've got a headache', etc. To such a claim we may reply as follows:

(a) It cannot be the case that the proposition 'I am in pain' or the proposition 'I've got a headache' are incorrigible whenever they are uttered, i.e. that there could be no circumstances in which they could be false. It is true of such propositions, as it is of any other proposition, such as 'This is my hand', that the mere uttering of them does not guarantee their truth. It is the circum-stances under which such propositions are uttered which make them incorrigible, if they are incorrigible, not the status of the propositions in themselves. Part of the situation, of course, is that we must be able to discount, for instance, the possibility of insincerity on the part of the speaker.

(b) We must not construe 'I am in pain' as shorthand for 'I know that I am in pain', any more than we should construe reports about what I see or hear, for example 'I saw an elephant in the High Street' as shorthand for 'I know that I saw . . .', as if reports of how I feel or what I see were knowledge claims. It makes no sense in my case, if I feel pain, to try to find out if I am in pain; but since I cannot feel your pain, it is significant for me to try to find out whether you are in pain. 'I know that he is in pain' can, therefore, be a significant knowledge claim: 'I know that I am in pain' cannot. There are no occasions for the use of such expressions as 'I know that I am in pain', except as an emphatic way of asserting 'I *am* in pain', or as a way of saying 'I feel pain'. But 'feeling pain' is not a *knowing* of anything. 'Knowing my headache' is not a possible synonym for 'feeling a pain in my head'. If I feel pain, I am in the strongest possible position for saying 'I am in pain', and unless you doubt my sincerity, there is no reason why you should not accept what I say. The proposition 'I am in pain', uttered by me when I feel pain, is 'incorrigible' in the sense that I need no evidence to assure me that I am in pain, or in the sense that it would be absurd for me to try to 'verify' that I am in pain. But, as we have seen earlier, there can be many sorts of propositions which are incorrigible in this sense. The conclusion which we should on no account draw is the conclusion that since I cannot feel your pain, since I may have to investigate whether you are in pain, I can never know that you are in pain simply because the proposition 'You are in pain' is not incorrigible in any sense.

My main contention, thus, is that there is no reason why we should restrict the use of 'I know' to propositions which are necessarily true or to empirical propositions which are deemed to be incorrigible, if there are any. Our everyday practice of claiming to know, and conceding other people's claims to know, the truth of contingent propositions remains unscathed. The mere fact that a proposition *could* be false does not, in itself, prevent us from knowing that it *is* true on a particular occasion, for example the proposition 'The coal bucket is empty' could be false on some occasions when uttered by somebody, but there can be other occasions when, to use Austin's forceful words (*op. cit.*, p. 115), we know that it is 'certainly, definitely, and un-retractably *true*'.

Before concluding this chapter, we should notice briefly two positions with which the view advanced above is in partial or total conflict. The first position is to the effect that there are two senses of knowledge to be distinguished, namely the 'weak' and the 'strong' senses. According to Professor Malcolm in *Knowledge and Certainty* (Englewood Cliffs, New Jersey: Prentice-Hall Inc., 1963, reprinted in Phillips Griffiths (ed.), *Knowledge and Belief* (O.U.P., 1967) pp. 69 ff.) the word 'know' is being used in its strong sense when 'a person's statement "I know that *p* is true" implies that the person who makes the statement would look upon nothing whatever as evidence that *p* is false'. The word is used in the weak sense when 'I am prepared to let an investigation (demonstration, calculation) determine whether the something that I claim to know is true or false.' Since Malcolm insists that the strong sense of 'know' is applicable to certain empirical propositions, such as 'Here is an ink-bottle', as well as to some necessary propositions, such as '$2+2 = 4$', and since he seems to accept that we can know the truth of propositions which *could have been* false, it is hard to see why he should adopt this half-way house position. The contrast to be drawn is surely not between what the speaker *is prepared* to accept as evidence and what he is *not prepared* to accept, but rather between the situation where the circumstances are such that there is no need to verify a proposition, for example 'Here is an ink-bottle', uttered by me when I am looking at it, and a situation where some tests may be required, such as Austin's example (*op. cit.*, pp. 118–19) where I verify your assertion that there is a telephone in the next room. The absence of tests in the one case and the need for tests in the other does not entail that we have two senses of 'know' or that our knowledge in the latter case is in any way enfeebled.

There remains the sceptic who will not accept the legitimacy of using the word 'knowledge' of empirical propositions on the grounds that, even in the most favoured cases, there is always the theoretical possibility of error, or, as it is sometimes said, it is always possible to doubt the truth of an empirical or contingent proposition. Some sceptical philosophers speak as if we had an unrestricted license to doubt, as if a person who makes a knowledge claim is always vulnerable but a person who doubts is never so. But the truth is that we have to have a reason for doubting something just as, usually, we have to have a reason for claiming to know something. One can always ask the sceptic, 'Why do you doubt that the coal bucket is empty after examining it carefully?' If he answers, 'Because I filled it only a short time ago', we can always take steps to remove the causes of his doubt. If he answers, 'I have no idea, but I still doubt it', we should not concede that he was doubting in any rational sense, and should pay him no heed. General theoretical doubt, or doubt based on nothing more than an uneasy feeling, is akin to neurosis and is universal in its scope; it can be directed upon the propositions of mathematics and logic just as much as on empirical propositions. We should think of it not as a particularly formidable form of reasonable doubt, i.e. doubt which is amenable to evidence, but as unreasonable doubt.

In conclusion, we must register a mild protest against the identification of empirical knowledge with 'certainty beyond reasonable doubt'. This half-apologetic phrase is objectionable if it is intended to suggest that empirical knowledge is good enough, but not quite up to the highest standards attainable in mathematics, for example. The phrase, 'certain beyond reasonable doubt', has its use in technical contexts, such as in legal contexts, where cast-iron certainty is unobtainable. But knowing that the coal bucket is empty after taking every care to see that it is, is knowledge at its best. After all, we learned the use of the word 'knowledge' in situations such as this and then transferred it to sophisticated situations such as those of logic and mathematics. Why not just call it knowledge?

6 Knowing as an Act

In previous chapters I have considered the attempts of some philosophers to link the notions of knowledge and infallibility by restricting the range of things which can be known to propositions which in no circumstances could be false. Thus we have seen that, on the more rigorous view, the possibility of achieving knowledge is restricted to necessary truths such as are to be found in logic and mathematics. On the less rigorous view, in addition to such necessary truths, some contingent propositions are included, namely those which are deemed to be incorrigible, such as propositions which describe our immediate sensations or feelings. We must now consider attempts to link the notions of knowledge and infallibility by restricting the procedures by means of which knowledge can be acquired to those which are foolproof or self-guaranteeing. Such attempts aim to eliminate the possibility of error by allowing only those procedures to count as 'ways of knowing' which are risk-free, as opposed to trying to eliminate error by restricting the things which can be known to propositions which could not be false.

Not all philosophers, however, who have sought to restrict ways of knowing to such risk-free procedures, agree on which procedures should be so designated. At various times, 'direct awareness', 'acquaintance', 'immediate apprehension', 'intuition', 'introspection' and 'deduction' have been cast to fulfil the role of error-free ways of knowing. Nor, indeed, has there been general agreement on the things which can be known by such procedures. Favoured candidates have been 'necessary truths', 'self-evident truths', 'axioms', 'facts', 'sense-data', 'universals' and 'mental states or events'. But some philosophers who have advocated the

75

claims of one or more of these allegedly self-guaranteeing procedures have not wished to reject all other procedures which are not
self-guaranteeing as possible sources of knowledge. Thus Russell,
as we shall consider in detail later, allows 'knowledge by description' (which is not self-guaranteeing) in addition to 'knowledge by
acquaintance' (which is self-guaranteeing). But even these
philosophers have given pride of place as 'ways of knowing' to
those procedures which are deemed to be incorrigible or free from
error. Other 'ways of knowing', if there are any, which may
involve the risk of error, are deemed to be 'secondary', and must
be based on or derived from the primary 'direct' ways of knowing
which *are* error-free.

Although there is no general agreement on the designation of
self-certifying 'ways of knowing', such attempts to link knowledge
and infallibility tend to exhibit certain common features. We shall
consider these features before attempting to answer the question
whether knowing can significantly be described as an 'act'.

There has been a persistent tendency to regard knowing something as an 'act' or 'activity' or 'experience'. Just as transitive
verbs such as 'to pick', 'to break' or 'to hit' take a direct object, as
in 'He picked the peas', 'He broke the window', 'He hit the table',
and, further, denote activities which occur at a particular time, so
'psychological verbs', i.e. verbs allegedly denoting mental activities, such as 'to think', 'to wonder', 'to infer', 'to assume', 'to
realise', 'to know', are assimilated to this pattern. They, too, are
taken to denote activities which occur at particular times and to
take direct objects. The basis of the assimilation is that the
grammatical analysis in terms of the distinction between 'act' and
'object' which applies to ordinary transitive verbs is taken to be
equally applicable to psychological verbs.

It is, of course, true that many such verbs, for example 'to
think', 'to realise', 'to conclude', 'to recall', appear to denote
activities which occur at particular times. But there are some
uses which clearly do not denote activities occurring at a particular time, such as 'He remembers the way to the theatre', 'He
believes that honesty pays', 'He knows the capital of Mexico'.
In none of these expressions is any reference being made to
the performance by someone of any act at any particular time,
as there is in such an expression as 'He broke the window'.
'He broke the window' refers to a dateable occurrence which
could be specified in answer to the question 'When?'; 'He knows

the capital of Mexico' clearly does not refer to any dateable occurrence, and the question 'When?' cannot significantly be answered. Further, the sense of the term 'object' seems to have changed in passing from transitive verbs such as 'to pick' to verbs such as 'to realise' etc. Whereas in the former case the object is expressed by nouns, as in 'He picked the peas', in the latter case the object has, normally, to be expressed by a 'that clause', as in 'He realised *that* the train was late', 'He concluded *that* he had lost his way', etc. Whereas it would be usual to regard the object of a transitive verb as a 'thing' or 'entity', for example 'window' in 'He broke the window', it would be stretching the terms 'thing' and 'entity' if we regarded '*that* the train was late' as a thing or entity. In the case of the verb 'to know', the assimilation to ordinary transitive verbs is made all the easier by the fact that, in one of its many uses, it is followed grammatically by a noun as a direct object, as in 'He knows Blackpool', 'He knew Churchill', as opposed to its propositional use, as in 'He knows *that* Paris is in France'.

The procedures listed above, such as acquaintance, intuition, direct awareness, apprehension, etc. are often regarded as synonyms of 'knowing' or as 'ways of knowing' and are all describable as 'acts' or 'activities'. The identification of such procedures with 'knowing', coupled with the predilection of some philosophers for 'active' or 'occurrent' uses of psychological verbs (i.e. those uses which appear to denote the occurrence of dateable acts such as realising, concluding, inferring), has encouraged the conclusion that knowing is primarily, if not exclusively, to be regarded as a 'cognitive act or activity'. On the pattern of transitive verbs, the distinction is drawn, it is thought with perfect propriety, between the 'act' or 'experience' of knowing and what is known. In brief, knowing is conceived as something which we *do*. If 'knowing that Great Britain is an island' is not quite like 'breaking the window', it is at least comparable with 'realising that the train was late' or 'concluding that he had lost his way', which, it is alleged, denote specifiable acts or activities, something which we *do*.

A development of the above view is that if a procedure is to count as an act of knowing, it must be 'direct' in the sense that the object of the act of knowing must be 'directly present to consciousness'. The object might, indeed, vary from one act of knowing to another. It might be a 'fact' or a 'truth', as in the case of intuition or immediate apprehension, or it might be a thing or perhaps a person, as in the case of acquaintance: whether it is a fact or a thing, it must be something of which we are 'immediately aware', something with which we can be directly confronted. 'Knowing' is thus conceived as a sort of inspection or apprehension of what is present to consciousness. One of the merits of such an account of knowledge, it has been claimed, is that it enables us to distinguish clearly and sharply between knowledge and belief. Thus the contrast is drawn between knowing, as something which is direct and immediate, and belief, which is indirect and mediate. In the case of knowledge, a fact is directly present to my consciousness: in the case of belief, what is present is not a fact but something else which corresponds with the fact if the belief is true, and does not correspond with the fact if the belief is false (Cf. H. H. Price, 'Some Considerations about Belief', *Proceedings of the Aristotelian Society*, Vol. 35 (1934–5), reprinted in Phillips Griffiths (ed.), *Knowledge and Belief*, (O.U.P. 1967) especially pp. 41–2.)

We thus have two views: (a) that knowing is always an act, or that acts of knowing are to be regarded as primary and other possible forms of knowledge as secondary, and (b) that knowing is a direct relationship to a fact or thing which is immediately present to consciousness. The conjunction of these two views, in the eyes of many philosophers has made necessary the conclusion that knowing is an activity which is immune from the possibility of error. The dictum 'knowledge cannot be mistaken' is now satisfied, not by excluding as possible objects of knowledge all propositions except those which could not be false, but by excluding as possible 'ways of knowing' all activities except those which are self-certifying or self-guaranteeing. Knowing is conceived of as something which is 'infallible' in contrast with belief, which is described as 'fallible'. We have found a meeting-place for what I regard as two of the principal myths in much of the traditional theory of knowledge, namely the Infallibility Thesis and what may be termed the Occurrent Thesis. Both are exemplified in such pronouncements as 'Knowledge is the infallible apprehension of a fact'.

My view is that this whole approach to the concept of knowledge is fundamentally mistaken. I tried to show in earlier chapters that if a proposition is only contingently true, i.e. could have been false (such as 'the coal bucket is empty'), this does not in itself prevent someone on occasion from knowing (as opposed to believing) that it is true; the restriction of the possibility of knowledge to necessary truths was seen to be based on a misconception of what is involved in the dictum 'knowledge cannot be mistaken'. In a complementary way, we do not have to accept the barren conclusion that knowledge is impossible simply because the customary ways of seeking to acquire knowledge, namely observation, calculation, reasoning, experimenting, etc. are not exempt from error. Nor is it necessary to introduce or invent unfamiliar methods such as 'apprehension', 'acquaintance', 'rational intuition', etc. as foolproof ways of knowing in order to satisfy the dictum that knowledge cannot be mistaken. The search for incorrigible cognitive acts is based on the simple fallacy of thinking that we can be right only where we cannot in principle be wrong. It is as if someone ruled out the possibility of anyone arriving at his destination because all methods of travelling are subject to accidents, or ruled out the possibility of ever finding something because there are no ways of searching which are inherently bound to succeed. Nothing is lost by dispensing with the search for ways of knowing which are in principle foolproof. Success, in the sense of getting into the position of knowing something, is not ruled out by the fact that learning is a 'fallible' process.

A further consequence of the conjunction of regarding knowing as an infallible, self-certifying act and the object of an act of knowing as something which is directly present to consciousness is that, whenever we know something, we must know that we know it. Thus, according to H. A. Prichard (*Knowledge and Perception* (Oxford: The Clarendon Press, 1950), reprinted in Phillips Griffiths, *op. cit.*, p. 61), 'We must recognise that whenever we know something we either do, or at least can, by reflecting, directly know that we are knowing it . . .' This reflexive characteristic of knowledge, however, has puzzled many philosophers, inasmuch as it seems to generate an unwelcome regress: if, whenever I know something, I must know that I know it, does it not also follow that I must know that I know that I know it . . . ? How, philosophers have puzzled, can the regress be halted once it starts? Why, we may add, if knowing is self-certifying in this way, does it happen sometimes that we have to confess that we were in error when we sincerely claimed to know, and have to withdraw the claim to knowledge? How, on such a view as this, could we find a place for such familiar expressions as 'I thought I knew . . .'? This puzzle, however, arising from the reflexive character of knowing, cannot be solved before we consider the propriety of regarding knowing as an 'act'. This we are now in a position to do.

Three main varieties of knowledge are commonly distinguished, namely (a) knowing how to do something: knowing how to swim, knowing how to mend a fuse, knowing how to argue, etc. (b) knowledge of truths or facts (so-called propositional knowledge): knowing that Great Britain is an island, knowing that two and two make four, etc. The verb 'to know' is followed, grammatically, by a substantival clause; (c) knowledge of things, as opposed to knowledge of truths, where, grammatically, the verb 'to know' is followed by a substantive, as when we speak of knowing people, places and things. Which, if any, of these varieties can properly be regarded as acts of knowing, or as involving acts of knowing?

It is clear, in the first place, that the description of knowing as an act is inappropriate in respect of knowing how to do something. If I myself say 'I know how to swim', or if someone says of me 'He knows how to swim', in neither case is reference being made to an act which is now occurring; I am not saying that I am doing something now, nor is the speaker crediting me with the doing of something now. On the contrary, expressions such as 'I know how to swim', or 'He knows how to swim', far from being descriptions of presently occurring acts, refer to a claim to possess, or the crediting of a claim to possess, a certain long-standing skill or ability. This, and the fact that I can properly be credited with knowing how to swim when I am not actually swimming, has led philosophers to introduce a distinction between those words which indicate 'acts', such as 'picking', 'breaking' or 'hitting', and those words which indicate 'dispositions', such as 'knowing how to swim', 'believing in the medicinal properties of brandy'. Moreover, nouns as well as verbs may have a dispositional use; they may indicate dispositional properties which things or people may possess, such as 'generosity', 'serenity', 'malleability'.

This distinction between 'acts' and 'dispositions' has not been clearly drawn, and may well mislead us. It may do so in at least two ways: firstly, the use of the single term 'disposition' to cover such disparate things as abilities, skills, moods, physical properties, etc. may well mask differences between them which are significant, or it may suggest that they have some unique property in common in virtue of being all described as 'dispositions'. Secondly, with particular reference to knowledge, the substitution of 'knowing is a disposition' for 'knowing is an act' may encourage the mistaken belief that, if knowing is not a mental act, it must be some sort of 'mental state', so that to say of someone that he knows so-and-so is to be construed as giving a description of his 'state of mind', comparable with the way in which saying of someone that his liver is jaundiced is giving a description of the state of his body. But the distinction between the active and dispositional uses of certain words should not be taken as an acceptance of the legitimacy of the disjunction 'knowing is either a mental act or a mental state'. All that need be intended by it is to call attention to the fact that many verbs are not used to refer to the present occurring of any action. 'He is swimming' does describe the doing of something now, but in the expression 'He knows how to swim', the words 'knows how to' do not describe the present doing of anything.

It is sometimes claimed that even if the verb 'to know' is used in a dispositional sense in such an expression as 'He knows how to swim', there must also be a corresponding 'occurrent' or 'active' use, since a disposition can only be acquired by the performance of certain acts, and when acquired will manifest itself in the performance of further acts. It is, of course, true that a skill or ability, such as knowing how to swim, is acquired by a series of acts and will normally display itself in further acts, but neither the preliminary nor the subsequent acts will be 'acts of knowing'. I acquire the ability to swim not by performing acts of knowing how to swim, but by a process of learning, by jumping into the water and trying to co-ordinate my movements and my breathing, etc., and I show that I have acquired the ability not by acts of knowing how to swim, but by getting from one place to another in the water without sinking. There is, thus, no place for 'acts of knowing' in the analysis of 'knowing how to do something'. 'He is learning how to swim' is a possible description of what someone is now doing: 'He is knowing how to swim' has no currency. In the case of 'knowing how', therefore, there is no 'active' or 'occurrent' use corresponding to the dispositional use of the verb 'to know'.

Similar considerations apply to our knowledge of truths or facts, which, too, is dispositional knowledge. My knowing that Great Britain is an island, or that two and two make four, does not indicate the performance of any act which is occurring now. I can quite properly claim to have known for thirty years that Great Britain is an island, and further, can properly claim to know it even when I am not attending to the question. Of course, in many cases of such factual knowledge, my knowledge was acquired as the result of an act or series of acts, and it may well exhibit itself in further acts. But as with knowing how to do something, though not perhaps so obviously, there is no place for 'acts of knowing', either as antecedents or as consequents. I came to know that Great Britain is an island by, for example, reading it in a text book or by hearing it said in a classroom or by sailing around it in my yacht. These activities represent not ways of knowing but ways of learning something. Once this item of knowledge is acquired, i.e. once I have learned it, I may show that I know it by, for example, giving the right answer in response to a question, or by correcting someone who said that Great Britain was a peninsula, or in a variety of ways, none of which is an 'act of knowing that Great Britain is an island'. Thus neither the expression 'I know that Great Britain is an island' nor 'He knows that Great Britain is an island' refers to the performance of any act which is occurring now. 'He is knowing that Great Britain is an island' is not a possible description of what someone is now doing.

Our knowledge of things, as opposed to our knowledge of truths, is also dispositional rather than occurrent. My knowledge of Blackpool cannot be described in terms of an act or event which is occurring now: I acquired it by visiting Blackpool and wandering around, and may show my knowledge of it by, for example, correctly identifying it if I pass through it. Once this knowledge is acquired, it tends to be retained, and one may be credited with its possession even when nothing relevant is being done. The same is true of our knowledge of things, for example my knowing what a mattock is. This knowledge, too, is dispositional and cannot be described as an event which occurs at a particular time. There may well have been an occasion which could be dated when I learned what a mattock is, but my 'knowing what a mattock is' cannot be a dateable event. It isn't something which I can be described as doing now. Precisely the same considerations apply to my knowledge of people.

Although these varieties of knowledge, namely knowing how to do something, knowledge of facts and knowledge of things, have been discussed separately, it must not be supposed that they are three quite independent types of knowledge which may be found in isolation. Our knowledge of people, for example, is a very complex matter. It is likely to involve knowing facts about a person, being able to recognise him on meeting him, knowing how to deal with him if he is angry or in a panic, or, minimally, it may merely imply having met him socially. It is important to recognise (a) that there is no one single factor which 'really' constitutes 'knowing John', which must always be present, and (b) that over and above our factual knowledge, our ability to recognise him, our knowing how to deal with him, etc., there is no 'cognitive act' or 'experience' of 'knowing John'. In much the same way, our knowledge of places will normally involve a good deal of factual knowledge, some 'knowing how', for example knowing how to get to the City Hall from Queen Street, together with the ability to recognise the place if we unexpectedly find ourselves there. Or again, our knowledge of how to do something is not wholly unconnected with knowledge of facts. Thus someone who knows how to do a cover drive will usually be able to give some sort of description of how it is done, such as that the feet must be in a certain position when the ball is struck, etc.

Attempts have sometimes been made, mistakenly I think, to accord some sort of logical priority to one variety of knowledge over the others, or to reduce all varieties of knowledge to one type. Thus it has sometimes been thought that priority should be given to factual knowledge, even though knowing how to do something frequently occurs without the agent making any conscious assertions about what he is doing, or perhaps even being able to do so, such as someone knowing how to tie a bow tie. Knowledge of methods cannot be reduced to knowledge of facts without remainder, as Professor Ryle showed conclusively in *The Concept of Mind*, Ch. 2. The exercise of a learned skill or ability is different from and cannot be reduced to the possession of correct information. On the other hand, it is equally unprofitable to try to reduce knowledge of facts to knowing how to do something. This could be done only if we were prepared to stretch the meaning of 'knowledge of facts' so that it is equivalent to 'being disposed to act in certain ways', for example 'knowing that Paris is the capital of France' would have to be construed as 'knowing how to, or being able to give the right answer in response to the question "What is the capital of France?"'. But discovering a fact in a reference book is hardly to be described as acquiring a skill, like the ability to swim, though in order to learn facts I must no doubt exercise some skills or abilities, such as the ability to read. What emerges is the involvement of these two varieties of knowledge (knowing how and knowing that) with each other, not the intrinsic primacy of either. The involvement varies from situation to situation: sometimes the 'skill' sense is paramount, sometimes 'knowing that'. The question whether theory must always precede practice or practice always precede theory has no significant answer; they are intertwined.

The fact that it is unprofitable to try to reduce one variety to the other becomes clear if we reflect that not all the varieties of knowledge have exactly the same features. In the first place, some types of knowledge admit of degrees, whereas others do not. Thus we may appropriately ask someone how well he knows Blackpool, and he may reply that he knows it well or slightly. Or again, 'knowing how' admits of degrees: one's ability to ride a bicycle may be slight or very marked. On the other hand, we could not meaningfully ask someone how well he knew that Paris was the capital of France, nor could someone meaningfully assert that he knew slightly that Paris was the capital of France.

In the second place, the involvement of the various types of knowledge with the notion of truth differs from one to the other. The connection with truth is clearly seen in the case of knowledge of facts (e.g. knowing that Paris is the capital of France), but is remote or absent in the case of 'knowing how' (e.g. knowing how to tie a bow tie). This suggests that it is impossible to reduce one variety of knowledge wholly to another.

Thirdly, the connection with the notion of intelligence is different in relation to 'knowing how' and 'knowing that'. The traditional predilection for 'knowing that' as the paradigm of knowledge has suffered a severe blow from Professor Ryle's demonstration that the link between knowledge and intelligence is predominantly in terms of knowing how to do something rather than in terms of knowing that something is the case. The ability to learn and remember facts is, of course, a condition of the exercise of intelligence, but intelligence is manifested not merely or primarily in the possession of information but in the ability to make use of the information. The ability to draw valid conclusions from a set of premisses has more to do with the exercise of intelligence than the mere ability to recite the premisses themselves. All this has conclusively been established by Professor Ryle in *The Concept of Mind*, Ch. 2.

It would, however, be a mistake to conclude from the fact that the person who knows how to cook is the one who can produce palatable dishes rather than the one who can merely recite recipes, that this demonstrates the logical priority of 'knowing how' over 'knowing that'. Far less would such considerations prove that 'knowing that' can be reduced to 'knowing how' to do something. In a relatively simple situation such as knowing how to ride a bicycle, the involvement of 'knowing that' is minimal, and we might agree that it could be altogether absent. But in knowing how to argue, for instance, some 'knowing that', such as knowledge of the premises, is necessary. Or again, knowing how to get from Oxford to Cambridge necessarily involves some knowledge of facts. The involvement of 'knowing that' with 'knowing how' varies from case to case, and it is significant that in those instances of 'knowing how' where knowledge is particularly related to intelligence, for example knowing how to argue as opposed to knowing how to ride a bicycle, the involvement of 'knowing that' is greater. We should also note that it would be strange to regard knowing how to ride a bicycle, where the involvement of propositional knowledge is minimal or wholly absent, as the paradigm either of knowing how to do something or of knowledge in general.

The conclusion, then, which emerges from our discussion of the varieties of knowledge, namely knowing how to do something, knowledge of facts and knowledge of things, is that there is no place for the introduction of 'acts of knowing'. While it is generally agreed that the category of 'act' is not appropriate for classifying *all* instances of knowledge, belief, memory etc., inasmuch as there must be at least some uses which are dispositional, such as 'He knows the capital of Mexico', 'He believes in regular exercise', 'He remembers how to scull', it is still widely held that there must be active uses in addition to the dispositional ones. Thus, 'assenting to' is sometimes said to be the occurrent sense corresponding to the dispositional sense of belief: 'recalling' is sometimes introduced as the occurrent sense of memory.

So far as knowledge is concerned, it is recognised that there is no use in English for such expressions as 'I am knowing so-and-so', but to some philosophers it is just a linguistic accident that the verb 'to know' is not used in English in an active, occurrent sense. Such philosophers either identify knowing with other familiar procedures which are undeniably acts or processes, or give familiar words new technical uses so that the doctrine that there are acts of knowing can be maintained. Thus, on the one hand, some philosophers take a list of familiar occurrent procedures and try to pick out those which can be identified as 'acts of knowing' and those which cannot. Inquiring, wondering and deliberating, for example, are not regarded as acts of knowing: these are classified as 'thinking' rather than 'knowing'. But other acts or processes such as reasoning or inferring, the apprehension of universals and the apprehension of relations between things experienced, are said to be 'activities of knowledge' (Cf. Cook Wilson, *Statement and Inference*, (Oxford: The Clarendon Press, 1926) pp. 34–47, reprinted in Phillips Griffiths (ed.), *op. cit.*, pp. 16–27.) Remembering, realising, concluding, recognising, sensing and, sometimes, perceiving are other activities which have been identified as 'acts of knowing'. On the other hand, other philosophers have introduced familiar terms such as 'acquaintance' and 'intuition' and invested them with technical senses so that they can stand for 'acts of knowing'. We must examine both the attempt to introduce such technical notions and the attempt to identify familiar procedures with 'acts of knowing'. If we can show that there cannot be 'acts of knowing', we shall have shown *a fortiori* that there cannot be 'infallible cognitive acts'.

7 Acquaintance and Intuition

1 ACQUAINTANCE

The view that acquaintance is one of the main forms, if not the main form, of knowing, is associated particularly, though not exclusively, with Russell's well-known distinction between knowledge by acquaintance and knowledge by description. This is discussed at length by Russell in *Mysticism and Logic* (London: Longman, 1918) pp. 209 ff., and more concisely in *The Problems of Philosophy* (The Home University Library, 1912; Oxford University Press, 1946), Ch. 5. Not only does it form the basis of Russell's theory of knowledge: it is perhaps the most influential contemporary contribution to the subject. I shall discuss the doctrine as it is presented in *The Problems of Philosophy*.

Russell's main contentions may be summarised as follows. A distinction is drawn between knowledge of truths and knowledge of things. Knowledge of things is then subdivided into (a) knowledge by acquaintance and (b) knowledge by description. About knowledge by acquaintance, simply defined in terms of saying that we have acquaintance 'with anything of which we are directly aware', Russell makes the following claims: (1) acquaintance is logically independent of knowledge of truths, though it is admitted that in practice it is accompanied usually, and perhaps always, by knowledge of truths; (2) it occurs without the intermediary of any process of inference; (3) it is incorrigible; (4) it is the foundation of all knowledge, since all knowledge, whether of things or of truths, is based upon knowledge by acquaintance. The things with which we can be acquainted are (1) sense-data, such as the colour, shape, etc. of the table when I am seeing it; (2)

in memory, with what we have seen or heard; (3) in introspection, with my desire for food when I desire food, or, more generally, with 'the events which happen in my mind'; (4) in some sense with the self as opposed to our particular experiences; (5) universals, i.e. general ideas such as 'whiteness', 'diversity', 'brotherhood', etc.

In contrast, we have no direct knowledge of physical objects; our knowledge of them is restricted to knowledge by description, which consists in knowing truths about them. The table, for example, is 'the physical object which causes such-and-such sense-data'. This describes the table by means of the sense-data which are the things with which we are acquainted. We have no direct knowledge of the table itself: indeed, Russell says, the table is not, strictly speaking, known to us at all. Again, we know other people's minds only by description, since we cannot be acquainted with their contents.

One of the considerations which seems to have prompted Russell to draw this distinction between knowledge by acquaintance and knowledge by description was the realisation that, in some sense of the terms, some knowledge is 'direct' and some 'indirect'. In the minimal sense of 'direct', it may be granted that there must be direct knowledge, i.e. it is not possible for everything to be known at second hand, such as by hearsay; somebody must know something at first hand. Thus, in this minimal sense, we could say that Brutus knew Caesar 'directly', whereas I can know Caesar only 'indirectly'. But all that is implied by this admission is that Brutus actually saw Caesar, whereas I never did. The fact that Brutus saw Caesar and I have not does not imply that Brutus was able to enjoy a special cognitive relationship with Caesar which is denied to me, as if looking at Caesar in itself constituted an act of 'knowing Caesar', or if not Caesar himself, the sense-data 'caused by Caesar himself'. Nor does it imply that Brutus was thereby able to dispense with knowing truths about Caesar, or that Brutus's knowledge of Caesar was necessarily 'incorrigible' whereas mine is necessarily 'corrigible'. In order for Brutus to 'know Caesar', he would at least have to know 'that it was Caesar' whom he was looking at: he would have to identify him as Caesar, though, of course, he need not formally express his ability to do so in the propositional form 'That is Caesar'. The mere fact that he saw Caesar, that Caesar was 'directly present to his consciousness', does not exempt him in principle from the possibility of mis-identifying Caesar.

Thus, the opposition of direct and indirect knowledge in this case is not an opposition between two different sorts of knowledge, but between different circumstances in which something is learned, namely the presence of observation in one case and the absence of it in the other. Of course, the fact that Brutus saw (i.e. met) Caesar puts him in a better position to know facts about Caesar, such as what he looked like, how he behaved in a crisis, etc., and gave him a better opportunity to confirm his hunches about Caesar, such as whether he was ambitious, etc. But the greater availability of the evidence does not mean that Brutus stood in a special cognitive relationship to Caesar which both dispensed with knowledge of truths and was necessarily incorrigible. In much the same way, we can draw a contrast between the 'direct' reports of eye-witnesses and 'indirect' reports based on hearsay. But, again, this does not imply a distinction between two sorts of knowledge, the one dispensing with truths and the other restricted to knowledge of truths. *Both* are reports, i.e. both involve knowledge of truths, and both are 'corrigible'. The reports of bystanders are not accepted simply because they 'saw what happened'.

It is, however, clear that the confrontation envisaged by Russell was not merely that Brutus knew Caesar simply in the sense that he met him. Nor, obviously, does Russell just want to say that there is a difference between first- and second-hand knowledge. For him, 'direct' knowledge is taken to involve some kind of 'cognitive confrontation' between the knower and the 'object' which is known, whereas 'indirect' knowledge fails to achieve this relationship. This is shown by Russell's own example of our alleged acquaintance with sense-data. In a very significant passage he says:

> The particular shade of colour that I am seeing may have many things said about it—I may say that it is brown, that it is rather dark, and so on. But such statements, though they make me know truths *about* the colour, do not make me know the colour itself any better than I did before: so far as concerns knowledge of the colour itself, as opposed to knowledge of truths about it, I know the colour perfectly and completely when I see it, and no further knowledge of it itself is even theoretically possible (1912 ed., pp. 73–4).

What, then, is the experience of 'knowing the colour' which is direct, incorrigible and independent of description?

In the first place, 'knowing the colour' cannot be identified with just looking at it, since looking at something, whether a thing or a sense-datum, though it might be described as 'direct', is in no sense an 'incorrigible' activity. Nor is it in any sense a 'knowing of anything'. 'Knowing' implies at the least being right about something, whereas 'looking at' in itself does not imply doing anything correctly or incorrectly. 'He is looking at the picture' (which in itself implies neither success nor failure) cannot be accepted as synonymous with 'he is knowing the picture'. Further, 'looking at' something cannot be totally independent, either in theory or in practice, of descriptions, since 'looking at a colour', for example, necessarily involves knowing *that* it is a colour which I am looking at and not something else.

Secondly, 'knowing the colour' cannot be equivalent to 'knowing what the colour is', since this would necessarily involve descriptive knowledge of the sort 'knowing that it is brown'. Nor can it be equivalent to 'being able to identify the colour' or 'recognising the colour', since 'being able to identify' is not an 'experience' or 'act' but a skill or ability which involves a process of learning and which would be impossible without some factual knowledge being involved, as well as knowledge of how to use words correctly. Further, 'recognising the colour' cannot be a cognitive act which is wholly independent of descriptive knowledge since recognising anything necessarily implies recognising X as being a such-and-such. We must conclude that there can be no 'act' or 'experience' of 'knowing the colour' which does not, at the very least, require the introduction of recognition or identification of what it is, and which, therefore, entails some factual knowledge.

Both of Russell's main contentions must, therefore, be rejected, namely that there is a way of knowing which logically dispenses with factual knowledge and is in principle incorrigible. 'Acquaintance with sense-data' does not denote an infallible, non-descriptive mode of knowing. It is just as true of a sense-datum as it is of a physical object that it is not 'presented' or 'given' to us already labelled, that it has to be recognised as being what it is. Such recognition involves knowledge of the use of concepts and there is always the possibility of mis-description. We have already seen (Chapter 5) that incorrigibility cannot be achieved by the expedient of replacing statements about 'physical objects' by statements about 'sense-data'.

The considerations which have been advanced with regard to 'acquaintance' apply with equal force to such expressions as 'directly present to consciousness' and 'direct awareness', which are sometimes introduced as synonyms of 'direct knowledge'. Apart from calling attention to the fact that there are some differences between finding out about something which we are now observing and finding out about something which cannot be, or is not now being observed, these expressions do not denote any specific 'act of knowing'. Of course, it does not follow that anything which I say about something which is now being observed by me must be true, since there is always the possibility of mis-description and, indeed, of mis-statement. 'Acquaintance' and 'direct awareness' are illustrations of the totally mistaken picture of 'knowing' as if it were some kind of acceptance of, or inspection of, some object which is 'given' or presented, without even the intermediary of the use of concepts.

Russell's second example of acquaintance was that of memory, where we are said to be acquainted with what we have seen or heard. But memory is no better as an example of an error-free, description-free 'way of knowing'. Whether memory takes the form of retaining a skill which one has acquired (e.g. remembering how to swim) or of retaining a fact which one has learned (e.g. remembering the date of the Battle of Waterloo) or in being able to recall what one has experienced in the past (e.g. remembering what I was doing this time last week), in none of these is there any place for a present 'act of knowing'. The general answer to Russell is that memory in itself is never a 'way of knowing' anything: it merely represents the fact that one has retained what one has learned. Thus, to the question, 'How did you come to know, or discover, so-and-so?', the answer, 'by memory' is not a possible one. Memory cannot be ranged alongside observation, calculation, inference, etc. as 'ways' or 'methods' of discovery. To the specific question 'Does remembering involve either an act of acquaintance with a past event, or an act of acquaintance with a present event?', the answer must be in the negative, if by 'acquaintance' is meant a process or act of knowing which is occurring now. If I have learned something and have not forgotten it, I do not have to re-discover the original fact now. If I remember it, I just produce it. There is no gap between the original discovery (which was the result not of an 'act of knowing' but of a process of learning) and my present ability to remember which has to be filled by an 'act of knowing' or an 'act of acquaintance' now. Remembering just means being able to produce now what I have learned or experienced.

The further obvious point is that memory in most of its senses is dispositional rather than occurrent—for example my remembering how to swim or my remembering the date of the Battle of Waterloo. These dispositions are activated not by 'acts of knowing' but by acts of swimming or correctly answering the question of the date of the battle. If, on the other hand, all that is intended by the introduction of 'acquaintance' in connection with memory is not so much to invoke a mythical cognitive act as to insist that in order to remember the past we must be 'familiar with' what we have seen or heard, then this can be accepted with equanimity.

Another example of acquaintance which Russell offers is our knowledge of universals, but this, again, does not involve the introduction of an act of knowing. Our knowledge of universals, for example, of redness, is clearly dispositional rather than occurrent. It is not at all like the inspection of, or apprehension of, a strange entity, but rather a complex, including knowing how to use words and being able to recognise instances of the universal. In no sense can our knowledge of 'redness' be wholly free of descriptive knowledge.

Russell's final example, namely our knowledge of our mental states or mental happenings, does not require us to postulate an incorrigible act of knowing. It may well be conceded that there is a sense in which it is true to say that, if I have a pain, then I cannot help knowing that I have a pain, that if I am hungry, then I cannot help knowing that I am hungry. But this should not be construed as conceding that 'knowing that I have a pain' involves a cognitive act of 'apprehending the fact that I have a pain'. As Professor Ayer remarks in *The Problem of Knowledge* (Penguin Books, 1956) p. 21, 'my knowing that I am having the experience is just my having it and being able to identify it ... To say that the experience itself is cognitive is correct, though perhaps misleading, if it is merely a way of saying that it is a conscious experience.' But this is not the sense of 'knowledge of our mental states' which Russell's doctrine of acquaintance requires. He is claiming that in addition to my feeling hungry or happy, there is such an experience as 'knowing my hunger' or 'knowing my happiness' over and above knowing *that* I am hungry, etc., a form of knowing which is logically independent of any knowledge of truths. But even if a sense could be attached to an expression such as 'knowing my hunger' which is different both from 'feeling my hunger' and 'knowing *that* I am hungry', Russell's criteria of 'acquaintance' still could not be satisfied. Mental states or happenings do not identify themselves any more than sense-data do.

I conclude, therefore, that the introduction of 'acquaintance' as a technical notion to stand for some instantaneous, direct, incorrigible act which is logically independent of knowledge of truths is mistaken. The notion of acquaintance has, indeed, a perfectly good sense in everyday life where we talk of being acquainted with people, places and things. But the ordinary use does not denote a unitary act or activity, but is a complex of 'knowing·that' and 'knowing how'—being acquainted with a person involves knowing facts about him, knowing how he behaves, being able to recognise him, etc., and is thus not in any sense logically independent of descriptive knowledge. Nor does the ordinary sense of acquaintance imply incorrigibility. The denial of the propriety of introducing the technical sense does not in any way imply a denial of the appropriateness of the ordinary sense of the term, of talking about being acquainted with people, places and things. The trouble arises when philosophers invest familiar terms with technical meanings which have little or no relation to their customary use. Thus there is nothing in the ordinary use of 'acquaintance' to suggest that it is some sort of cognitive act, some sort of inspection or confrontation with something which is 'directly presented to consciousness', nor is there the suggestion that it is an independent type of knowing which is different both from 'knowing that' and 'knowing how', and logically independent of both.

2 INTUITION

The other main candidate for consideration as an 'act of knowing' is intuition. Here, again, we have a term which is familiar in everyday life but which philosophers have invested with technical meanings which bear little relation to the customary use of the term. Thus, some philosophers have conceived of intuition as a positive act of knowing which is incorrigible. Descartes, for instance, regarded it as 'the conception of an unclouded and attentive mind, conception which is so distinct and so effortless that no doubt remains of what we comprehend' (*Regulae* I). Everyone, he asserts, can see by intuition that he exists, that he thinks, that the triangle is bounded by only three lines, etc.

Intuition, I believe, has wrongly been introduced as an inexplicable, unchallengeable act of knowing: it denotes, not the occurrence of a positive, uncommon act, but the absence of ordinary, familiar procedures. This can be seen by considering what exactly philosophers seem to have intended by its introduction. Of the many senses of the term which are current, we may select the following:

(1) To say that a truth is known by intuition is intended to call attention to the fact that not everything which we know has been arrived at by a process of inference. 'Intuitive' used of a proposition in this sense means 'uninferred'. This contention must, of course, be accepted, since it is logically impossible that every proposition which we claim to know could be the conclusion of an inference. Obviously, in any inference, if there is a conclusion, some propositions must serve as premisses which are themselves uninferred. Further, in the case of any individual, there will be many propositions the truth of which he has discovered without the need of inference, for example, the proposition that he himself exists. So much may be granted. But to say of any proposition that it is arrived at without inference does not in the least guarantee its truth; speed does not in itself rule out the risk of error. I may accept that 18 and 18 make 36 without taking any intermediate steps, but this does not eliminate the possibility of error. If I have learned my multiplication tables pretty well, I may be able to conclude that 9 multiplied by 9 makes 81 without any calculation, but I may also slip up and go for 99. Secondly, 'intuitive', in this sense of being uninferred, is not the description of a particular type of proposition, it is not the inherent property of any proposition. The same proposition can be intuitively known by me and known as the result of inference by you, as may be the case in the above mathematical examples. Thus, from the obvious point that not all truths can be deduced, nothing follows immediately about the superior nature of non-deduced truths, and we cannot conclude that there is a special class of propositions which are intrinsically non-deduced or intuitively known.

There is thus no justification for saying that some truths could be known only by inference and that others cannot be known by inference. Even if we were to conclude, as many have contended, that there must be some 'basic' propositions which are uninferred, the mere fact that they are uninferred does not guarantee their truth. Further, to say that a proposition is accepted as true without inference is not to say that it is arrived at by means of some positive act of intuition. 'Uninferred' denotes the *absence* of a familiar procedure not the *presence* of an unfamiliar one. To say, for example, of a proposition that it is 'self-evidently true' is precisely to say that *no* procedure is required, apart from an examination of the symbols alone.

(2) The description of a proposition as 'intuitive' sometimes refers to the fact that we do not ask for or require any justification of it in a particular case. There are, of course, many occasions when we are prepared to accept the truth of a proposition without asking the person who propounds it to provide justification in the form of rehearsing how he arrived at it or providing the evidence on which he would justify it if pressed. Normally, if you tell me something in everyday life, for example that you have lost your watch, that you have just woken up, etc., I will not question your statement or ask you to justify it. But the fact that a proposition is accepted on occasion without calling for a justification does not in the least guarantee its truth, nor does it mean that the proposition is thereby deemed to be incorrigible. To say, therefore, of a proposition that it is 'intuitively known', in the sense of being accepted without being justified, is not the description of a specific procedure or act of 'knowing a truth directly', and we are not tied to a static conception of a proposition as always and intrinsically 'intuitive'. The same proposition, accepted now without justification, might in different circumstances have to be justified.

(3) The adjective 'intuitive' applied to a proposition sometimes implies the absence of doubt. 'Intuitive', in this sense, is equivalent to 'indubitable'. But, here again, none of the desired consequences follow. The fact that someone finds it impossible to doubt the truth of a given proposition is no guarantee of its truth: the absence of doubt does not confer infallibility or incorrigibility on a proposition. Further, any proposition, even a false one, may well be regarded by someone at some time as 'indubitably true'. Much as in the case of the other senses discussed above, the *absence* of doubt is not to be construed as indicating the *presence* of some faculty or way of knowing which is of such a nature that its mere occurrence guarantees the truth of what is alleged to be known.

Intuition is not a positive procedure, some instantaneous, unchallengeable way or act of knowing; it is not an 'infallible seeing of a truth': to introduce the term is to indicate the absence of familiar procedures, such as inference, some procedure of justification or the absence of doubt. I am not, of course, suggesting that we should abandon the term 'intuition' either in philosophical contexts or in everyday life. Since it is true that we frequently get into the position of knowing something without having to reason or infer or justify ourselves, there is no reason why we should not say that we got into that position by 'intuition': this is acceptable provided that we are not claiming that we have performed some 'cognitive act', the mere occurrence of which guarantees its infallibility.

3   KNOWLEDGE AS AN ACT

I conclude, therefore, that there is no good reason for accepting the technical notions of acquaintance and intuition as providing instances of incorrigible 'acts of knowing'. There remains, however, the possibility referred to at the end of Chapter 6 that familiar, non-technical processes such as reasoning or inferring or calculating or observing or remembering could be assimilated to 'acts of knowing'.

It is, surely, obvious that the straight identification of any of these with 'knowing' is impossible, if only for the reason that inferring, observing, etc. are all activities which may be incorrectly as well as correctly done, whereas 'knowing something', if it ever occurred as an act, would necessarily have to be successful. 'Remembering' we have already dismissed, since it is not a way of knowing but the retaining of what we have learned by a variety of methods. At the same time, although reasoning, calculating, observing, etc. are all activities which may be incorrectly done so that none of them constitutes an 'act of knowing', yet any one of them may on occasion, if correctly done, result in someone getting to know something. But we must not confuse the procedures of observing, inferring, etc. with the position I may get into as the result of their successful performance. If I make certain experiments, for example, I may get into the position of being able to assert that the atomic weight of tin is so-and-so, and be able to justify my assertion. I will express myself in the categorical form

'The atomic weight of tin is so-and-so', and not in the form 'I know that the atomic weight of tin is so-and-so'. If I use the form 'I know that . . .', which one would do only sparingly, I do so not to announce the occurrence of some mythical cognitive act, but to insist that I am in a position to justify the truth of what I am asserting. Nor, as we shall see in the next chapter, am I using that form of words to describe my 'state of mind'.

Similarly, to say of a person that he knows so-and-so is not to be reporting on some infallible activity which he is now performing: it is to say that he is in a position to justify his claim that a given proposition is true. The accounts of his calculations, observations, reasonings, etc. will be relevant to the justification which he may offer for making his claim. Thus, if someone claims that there is a lion in the garden and his claim is challenged, he may attempt to justify his claim by reference to what he has himself observed. His statements about his observations will not be statements about his 'knowings', but part of the justification of his claim. Accepting his justification is equivalent to crediting him with 'knowing that so-and-so is true'.

The truth is that 'knowing' is never something which we *do*: the verb 'to know' is not a 'doing' verb. 'Knowing' is neither an independent activity nor is it to be identified with activities such as reasoning, observing etc. which may result in a person being in the position of 'knowing that so-and-so is true', nor is it an activity which supervenes on activities such as observing, reasoning, etc.

Knowing is not an independent activity since there is nothing which is described by such an expression as 'He is busy knowing that Great Britain is an island'. In order to get into the position of knowing something, you have to do something else, such as calculate, reason, observe, look up a reference book, question an authority, experiment, etc. Knowing is not something which you can do just on its own. In this respect it resembles such a verb as 'being intelligent' which does not denote an independent activity, something which can be done on its own. To be intelligent you have to talk sensibly about something, solve equations, etc. That knowing is not something that we do may be demonstrated by noting that we cannot choose or decide to know. Whereas one can decide to try to find something out, can decide to learn German, etc., one cannot significantly say that someone can decide or choose to know something, for example decide to know the atomic weight of tin or choose to know how to cast a fly. Again, whereas we can request someone or perhaps order someone to make calculations or observations, we cannot order or request someone to know something. 'Knowing', then, does not represent an autonomous activity, either in the way in which such verbs as 'picking' and 'hitting' do, or verbs such as 'calculating', 'assuming', 'observing' or 'wondering'. It is not, therefore, just a linguistic accident that there is no place for such expressions as 'He is knowing so-and-so'; nor should we be deceived into thinking that there is such an activity as 'knowing' because some philosophers speak of acts of cognising, of intuitings, of apprehendings, etc.

We have already seen that 'knowing' cannot be identified with the procedures which may or may not result in a person being in the position of 'knowing that so-and-so is true', procedures such as observing, inferring, etc. 'Knowing' is not a generic term of which 'inferring', 'calculating', 'looking in a text book', 'experimenting', etc. are species.

Nor will it do to say that 'knowing' is an act or activity which supervenes on activities such as observing, etc. We saw in Chapter 3 (following Professor Ryle) that verbs such as 'to find', 'to arrive', 'to win' do not denote independent activities which supervene on activities such as searching, travelling and running: the function of an 'achievement verb' is not to indicate an additional, independent activity but to record the successful completion of 'task' activities. In much the same way, there is no place and no need for an 'act of knowing' or an 'act of apprehending a truth' to supervene, for example, on the successful performance of certain experiments: their successful performance puts me in the position of being able to claim with justification that the atomic weight of tin is so-and-so. My careful observation of what is going on in the garden in itself, without the imposition of any 'act of knowing', puts me in the position of being able to assert, and justify my assertion, that there is a lion in the garden. The verb 'to know' is never a 'doing' verb. Its function is rather to claim a certain status: when I say 'I know that so-and-so is the case', I am claiming to be in a position to justify the truth of what I assert, or when I say 'I know how to do so-and-so', I am claiming to possess a certain ability. When you say 'He knows that so-and-so is the case', you are conceding him the status of being able to justify what he asserts to be true, or conceding his claim to be able to do so-and-so, when you say 'He knows how to do so-and-so'.

The position is, then, that since there are no 'ways of knowing' or 'acts of knowing', there cannot be any 'incorrigible cognitive acts'. There are many procedures, such as calculating, observing, inferring, etc. which are not in themselves exempt from error, but which may nevertheless result in a person being in a position to make knowledge claims which are accepted. These procedures may, of course, be described as 'intellectual activities', but to describe them as such is not to say that they are 'cognitive' activities in the sense of being 'acts of knowing'. The fact that there are no 'ways of knowing' which are incorrigible and no methods of learning which are foolproof does not rule out the possibility of success: we are not debarred from ever being right because of the fact that we might have been wrong. The false picture of knowing as a procedure which must in principle be 'infallible' or 'incorrigible', i.e. a procedure where the possibility of error has necessarily been excluded, has resulted in the vain search for incorrigible acts such as 'acquaintance' and 'intuition'. Such a search is misguided because it makes the double mistake of regarding 'knowing' as something which we do and thinking that success is possible only if the impossibility of failure can be guaranteed. It is just as much a misunderstanding of what is implied by the dictum 'knowledge cannot be mistaken' as the attempt discussed in previous chapters to restrict knowledge to propositions which in no circumstances could be false.

It is remarkable that traditional theories of knowledge, such as those of Plato, Locke, Berkeley and Hume, and contemporary theories such as those based on Cook Wilson and Prichard, pay so little regard to the notion of learning, with which the concept of knowledge is so closely connected. One of the advantages of the contemporary emphasis on 'knowing how' as opposed to 'knowing that' is that it makes this connection clearer. The process of learning, such as learning how to drive a car, is a process where mistakes are naturally expected to occur. At some stage, which varies from person to person, we are prepared to concede that someone knows how to drive a car, that he has passed from the apprentice stage and has acquired a certain ability or skill. To credit someone with knowing how to drive is clearly not to assert that he has performed an act of knowing which supervenes on the process of learning. It is rather to say that he has got to the position of eradicating the mistakes which characterised his earlier efforts, etc. It is to grant him a certain status. The process of learning is not, of course, error-free, but this in no way prevents us from crediting someone at the appropriate time with now knowing how to do something. Much the same is true of 'knowing that'. We get to the position of knowing that so-and-so is the case by a process of learning which may vary greatly in duration from person to person and depending on the subject matter. Thus, someone may come to know that oak trees shed their leaves in winter as the result of personal observation, or he may accept it on the authority of someone whose credentials are impeccable, or he may read it in a respected text book. To say that he knows that oak trees shed their leaves in winter is not to give a story about his observations or his researches in the text book: it is to credit him with having learned something with understanding, and with having remembered it. His observing or questioning is not to be described as a 'knowing of a fact directly present to his conscious-ness': it is the means which put him in the position of being able to assert with justification that a certain proposition is true.

The theory of knowledge has, in my view, had to pay a heavy price for disregarding the connection between knowledge and learning. The price is the assimilation of knowing to 'seeing', whether in the sense of 'perceiving by the senses' or in the sense of some internal 'intellectual seeing', for example in terms of instan-taneous acts of 'apprehending' or 'being acquainted with' or 'intuiting'. Those philosophers who have accepted the model of knowing as an act, and who have also fallen into the trap of thinking that we can be right about something only if we can eliminate even the theoretical possibility of being wrong, have naturally seen in such instantaneous acts as acquaintance and intuition the pattern of what knowledge should be. The concept of knowing has been married to the wrong partner.

8 Knowing as a Mental State

We come now to what I regard as the third myth in some of the traditional theories of knowledge, namely, that knowing is to be conceived of primarily in psychological terms. Much of the traditional doctrine can be expressed in terms of the disjunction 'knowing is either a mental act or a mental state' (and perhaps both). In Chapter 7 we have already rejected the first alternative, that knowing is a mental act; I now propose to show that the second alternative, that knowing is some sort of mental state or mental attitude, must also be rejected.

There are several versions of the doctrine that knowing should be conceived of in psychological terms, or that the category of 'mental state' is appropriately introduced in the analysis of knowing. I shall discuss the following three versions:

(1) To say that someone knows something is taken as giving a description of his state of mind or mental attitude towards a proposition. On the first view, this state of mind or mental attitude is reserved only for knowing and, being unique, nothing much can be said about it. It can, however, be identified by introspection and clearly distinguished from the mental attitude which is, or which accompanies, belief. The hall-mark of the mental state which is 'knowing something' is its 'infallibility'.

(2) The second version does not regard the mental state in question as specific to knowing or unique, nor as necessarily unanalysable. Knowing is now identified with the familiar notion of 'being sure'.

(3) The third version is significantly different from the first two in that knowing is not now *identified* with any specific mental state. On this view, 'being sure' is not synonymous with 'knowing', but

is said to be a 'necessary condition of knowing'. Thus, no one can truly be described as 'knowing that so-and-so is the case' unless he is himself 'sure' or 'confident' of the truth of what he is asserting. 'Knowing' thus involves 'being sure', though 'being sure' is only one of the conditions of 'knowing that so-and-so is true'.

The first two versions may be discussed together. It is obvious that 'knowing' cannot be equated with 'being sure' simply on the grounds that someone may be completely sure of something and yet be wrong. If 'being sure' is a characteristic of knowledge, it is equally a characteristic of error; indeed, the person who is in error about something is usually just as convinced as if he knew. We have to distinguish, I suggest, between error and false belief. By 'error', in this context, is meant not just the adoption of a belief, which is in fact false, by someone who is aware of the possibility that he may be wrong; I refer, rather, to the situation where someone is convinced that he is right to such an extent that he does not admit any doubt, and yet is wrong. If, therefore, we were to equate 'knowing' with 'being sure', we would not be able to distinguish between knowledge and error, in the defined sense.

Professor A. J. Ayer, in *The Problem of Knowledge* (Penguin Books, 1956), pp. 14–26, disposes of the view that knowing consists in being in some unique, infallible state of mind. He shows that 'there cannot be a mental state which, being as it were directed towards a fact, is such that it guarantees that the fact is so' (p. 19). The reason which he gives is that, even if someone is convinced of the truth of a proposition, it never follows logically that the proposition is true, though it might provide a reason for accepting it. There is no contradiction in asserting that someone is convinced of the truth of a proposition and simultaneously asserting that the proposition is false. What makes the proposition true is not that the person who asserts it is in a special state of mind, but that the facts are as they are stated to be. Thus, if someone is sure that Paris is the capital of France, the proposition 'Paris is the capital of France' is not made true by his being sure of it, but by the fact that Paris *is* the capital of France. But if the doctrine that knowing simply consists in being in a unique, infallible state of mind were true, then the mere fact that one was in that state of mind would be a sufficient condition for having knowledge. Further, we would not credit someone with knowing that a given proposition was true, however strongly he protested that he 'was sure', if we had reason to suspect that he had arrived at the truth by accident, or by guessing, or as the result of an invalid argument. Since there is no intrinsic connection between being in a certain state of mind and being right, the identification of 'knowing' with 'being sure' would miss the essential element in knowledge, namely that knowledge necessarily implies being right about something. This consideration applies whether knowing is equated with 'being sure' or whether it is identified with some unique state of mind which is alleged to be proprietary to knowledge.

In spite of these considerations, the view that to say 'I know' of myself or to say 'he knows' of someone else is, at least in part, to give a description of a state of mind or mental attitude, has been widely held, and has been vigorously defended by Professor Jonathan Harrison in his paper, 'Knowing and Promising' (*Mind*, Vol. 71 (1962) 443–57; reprinted in Phillips Griffiths (ed.), *Knowledge and Belief* (Oxford University Press, 1967) pp. 112–26). Professor Harrison brings out clearly some of the assumptions about knowledge which he thinks most philosophers would have taken for granted until recently. I shall try to summarise his account.

According to Harrison, the following would have been accepted about the statement 'I know she will be late':

(a) Anyone who said it would be saying something which was true or false.

(b) The statement 'I know she will be late' is different from the simple statement 'She will be late'. If the former were true, the latter must be true, but the latter could be true and the former false.

(c) If I say 'I know she will be late', and someone says of me 'He knew she would be late', the same proposition would be asserted by both. It could not be the case that one proposition was true and the other false.

(d) When I say 'I know she will be late', or when someone says of me 'He knew she would be late', what is being asserted is something about my 'mental attitude' towards the proposition 'She will be late'. The natural assumption is that since there are some true propositions which I know and others which I do not, the difference between knowing some and not knowing others lies in me, in my 'mental attitude' to these propositions, or in my 'state of mind'. Similarly, the difference between my knowing some propositions to be true and merely believing others to be true is to be explained as a difference in my 'state of mind'.

Professor Harrison adds that these assumptions, which had been taken for granted 'until recently', had been threatened by some of the contentions made by Professor J. L. Austin in his paper 'Other Minds' (*Proceedings of the Aristotelian Society*, Supplementary Vol. xx (1946), reprinted in *Philosophical Papers*, 2nd ed. (Oxford Paperbacks, 1970)). Two contentions in Austin's paper, if accepted, would mean that all the traditionally made assumptions listed above are wrong, namely that 'I know' is not a *descriptive* phrase, and that 'I know' functions in a parallel way to 'I promise'. This would be so for the following reason. When I say 'I promise', I am not *describing* the occurrence of any event: I am actually *doing* something, namely 'binding myself to others'. If we press the parallel, when I say 'I know', I am not *describing* the occurrence of any event or *describing* my state of mind or mental attitude. In Austin's words, 'saying "I know" . . . is *not* saying "I have performed a specially striking feat of cognition, superior, in the same scale as believing and being sure, even to being merely quite sure" . . . When I say "I know", I *give others my word*: I *give others my authority for saying* that "*S* is *P*"' (p. 99). If, then, 'I know' is comparable in this way with 'I promise', it will follow that no one saying 'I know' will be saying anything capable of being true or false, nor will there be any special state of mind which is described by the words 'I know' or 'he knows'. Harrison appears to believe, as against Austin, that when I say, 'I know so-and-so', I am making a *statement about myself* which is capable of being true or false (cf. *Knowledge and Belief*, p. 118) or 'stating a fact about myself' (p. 125).

In his article, Professor Harrison shows that there are many differences between saying 'I know' and saying 'I promise'—more, indeed, than Austin seems to have allowed. It may well be that Austin pressed the parallelism between 'I know' and 'I promise' too far, or failed to see that there are significant differences between the two expressions. It is, however, of crucial importance to show that, even if the parallel between 'I know' and 'I promise' has to be dropped, Harrison's conclusion that 'I know' states a fact about myself, or describes my mental state, does not necessarily follow.

The reason why the conclusion does not follow is that there are many ways in which expressions which are unlike 'I promise' can still fail to be descriptive, in the sense of saying something which is true or false. Of course, if I say 'I know that Paris is the capital of France', or if someone says of me 'He knows that Paris is the capital of France', it is correct to say, loosely and vaguely, that 'something is being said about me'; but it does not follow that something true-or-false is being said about my 'state of mind' or 'mental attitude'. When someone 'says something about me', there is a wide range of things which he may be doing, for example evaluating my conduct, disparaging my mathematical abilities, praising my golf swing, etc., as in 'He behaves better in committees than he used to', 'He has no idea how to multiply fractions', 'He has a pleasing, rhythmical swing'. None of these remarks could fairly be taken as saying something true-or-false about my 'state of mind'. Similarly, the fact that 'knowing' is unlike 'promising' does not mean that saying of someone that he knows something is, thereby, necessarily making an assertion, which can be true or false, about his mental attitude. From the two negative premisses, ' "I promise" is not descriptive' and ' "I know" is not like "I promise" ', no positive conclusion follows, certainly not ' "I know" is descriptive'. On the other hand, it must be conceded that, although Austin's position may be presented as an argument which is formally valid, we are not thereby forced to accept his conclusion that 'I know' is not descriptive. Thus, whereas the conclusion ' "I know" is not descriptive' follows formally from the conjunction of the premisses, ' "I promise" is not descriptive' and ' "I know" is like "I promise" ', the conclusion may still be false since one or more of the premisses may be false. My own view is that Austin's comparison of 'I know' with 'I promise' was unfortunate, but that he was perfectly right in warning us against the 'descriptive fallacy', if by that he meant the fallacy of thinking that 'I know' or 'he knows' are descriptions of a mental state or mental attitude which I or someone else may be in.

In his criticism of Austin, Harrison points out what he regards as one of the differences between 'I know' and 'I promise', namely that whereas someone who says 'I promise' is thereby promising, someone who says 'I know' is not thereby knowing. He is, Harrison says, 'simply claiming that he knows' (*op. cit.*, p. 118). In this, I think, Harrison is mistaken, and it is clear that this is not the interpretation of 'I know' which Austin intended. When he offered an equivalent for 'I know', he did not say, 'I give others my authority for *claiming to know* that "*S* is *P*" ', but 'I give others my authority for *saying that* "*S* is *P*" '. While I think it is correct to say that 'I know that so-and-so is the case', in a suitable context, represents the making of a claim, it is mistaken to regard it as equivalent to 'claiming to know that so-and-so is the case', since this would be merely circular. When someone says 'I know that so-and-so is the case', what he is in fact doing is claiming that a certain proposition is true and that he has adequate reasons for asserting its truth.

Two questions, therefore, remain to be answered, namely whether 'saying "I know"' is equivalent to 'claiming to know', and whether 'I know' is a description of my state of mind.

The fact that 'saying "I know"' is not always equivalent to 'claiming to know', and particularly that it is not equivalent to 'claiming to know' when used in such expressions as, 'I know *that* so-and-so is the case', can be seen by a study of the following illustrations:

Example 1. The teacher at school asks the class: 'Does anyone know the date of the Battle of Waterloo?' Tommy says '*I* know the date of the Battle of Waterloo.' The points to be noticed here are:

(a) No assertion is made about the date of the battle.

(b) Although Tommy is 'saying something about himself', it does not necessarily follow that Tommy is saying something about his state of mind or mental attitude to a proposition.

(c) Tommy might properly be described as 'claiming to know something'.

(d) It would not make sense for Tommy to say 'I know the date of the battle' except in answer to such a question as, 'Does anyone know . . . ?' That is, his statement needs a context in order to be significant.

Example 2. The teacher asks 'What was the date of the Battle of Waterloo?' Tommy says 'The date of the Battle of Waterloo was 1815'. The teacher, suspecting that Tommy may have been guessing, asks 'Are you sure?', to which Tommy indignantly replies, 'I *know* that the date was 1815'. The points to be noticed are:

(a) It would have been inappropriate for Tommy to have said in reply to the question 'What was the date . . . ?', 'I know that the date was 1815', but appropriate to say 'I know that . . .' in reply to the question 'Are you sure?' These examples show, I think, how dangerous it is to try to understand the use of the expression 'I know' out of the context of discourse. In isolation, 'I know she will be late', or 'I know the date of the Battle of Waterloo', might well appear to be just making a straightforward, factual, true-or-false remark about me.

(b) Tommy's first reply, 'The date of the Battle was 1815', is an assertion about the date of the battle, something which can be true or false. This assertion remains in the second answer, 'I know that the date of the battle was 1815'. At the same time, there is clearly a difference between Tommy saying 'The date of the Battle of Waterloo was 1815', and saying 'I *know* that the date was 1815'. In the second, he is, loosely, 'saying something about himself' which he is not doing in the first. Are there, then, two assertions which can be true or false in the second answer, and only one in the first, i.e. the assertion of the date of the battle and the further assertion about Tommy's state of mind? No. The force of the second answer is that Tommy is claiming that the proposition 'The date of the battle was 1815' is true, and further that he has good reasons for asserting it as a truth. If the teacher, after further inquiry, should add, 'Yes, you do know the date of the battle', this would not be a true-or-false statement about Tommy's mental state: it would be equivalent to conceding that what he had said was correct and that he had given adequate justification for his assertion, perhaps that he had just read it in a reputable text book. In the first example, where Tommy says '*I* know the date of the battle', he is claiming that *he is able to give* the right answer: in the second example, when he says 'I *know* that the date was 1815', he is claiming that *he has given* the right answer, and that he can justify it.

(c) Thus, treating 'I know' as equivalent to 'claiming to know' is appropriate, if at all, only in answer to such a question as 'Does anyone know the date of the Battle of Waterloo?', where someone says '*I* know the date . . .'. It is not appropriate as equivalent to 'I know *that* the date was 1815'. This remark is not to be regarded as 'claiming to know' but as 'claiming that *p* is true', and that one is in a position to assert it as a truth, i.e. one could, if required, justify one's asserting it as a truth.

Thus, in the two propositions 'The date of the battle was 1815' and 'I know that the date was 1815', the only assertion which is true or false is 'The date of the battle was 1815'. The additional factor which is present in the second and absent in the first is whether Tommy had the right to assert it as a truth, or was in a position to assert it as a truth, i.e. whether he had adequate reasons for asserting it or whether he was just guessing, etc. The considerations which would induce the teacher to concede that Tommy knew the date of the battle would be the correctness of his answer (which is, of course, essential) and the strength of the support which he is able to give it, not any protestations which Tommy might make to the effect that he was 'sure' or that he was in some unique state of mind which he, and only he, could inspect. Of course, there would be no need for the teacher to infer from the correctness of Tommy's answer and the quality of its support (which are open to public scrutiny) either to the occurrence of some private mental act of knowing on Tommy's part or to the presence of some unique, infallible state of mind. The question of his mental state or mental attitude does not arise. The judgement whether Tommy knows or not could be made from the above-mentioned publicly observable facts. *A fortiori*, therefore, it would be absurd to say that the teacher *must* make such an inference before conceding Tommy's claim.

The question 'Does Tommy know the date of the battle?' is thus a psychological question only in the harmless sense that it is a question about Tommy, a question about a person. But it is not a psychological question in the sense that it is a request for a true-or-false story about Tommy's state of mind. This is particularly evident in the case of 'knowing how'. Thus, when I say, in a given context, 'I know how to mend a fuse', although I am 'saying something about myself', I am neither reporting the occurrence of a 'cognitive act or event' nor describing my mental state or condition. I am claiming that I can do so-and-so, not claiming to know how to do so-and-so. Similarly, if someone says of me 'He knows how to mend a fuse', he is admitting that I am able to do so-and-so. 'Knowing that', in this respect, is no different from 'knowing how'. When I say 'I know that...' I am neither reporting an event nor describing a mental state, whether a unique mental state or my 'being sure'. The force of such a remark, which must be given a context to be significant, is to claim that I have given the right answer and that I am justified in asserting it as a truth.

A further point about the question 'Does Tommy know the date of the Battle of Waterloo?' is its deceptive simplicity. It sounds as if it were a request to establish a fact about Tommy, a clear-cut, once-for-all, true or false conclusion about Tommy, comparable with the questions 'Was Tommy born at sea?' or 'Does Tommy live in Cardiff?' One might, therefore, be inclined to suppose that even if the question 'Does Tommy know the date . . . ?' does not call for a true-or-false statement about Tommy's state of mind, yet it must call for a true-or-false statement about something. But the question is much more like the questions 'Is Tommy good at geometry?', 'Is Tommy better at golf than he is at sums?' or 'Does Tommy behave well at parties?' In other words, the question requires not a simple, true-or-false statement about Tommy, but an *assessment of*, or *judgement on*, what Tommy says. As we have seen, two things are required in order to answer the question 'Does Tommy know the date of the battle?' In the first place, we have to establish that the proposition which he claims to be true *is* true, i.e. that he says '1815' and not '1817' (which may be treated as establishing a fact), and secondly, we have to *assess* or *judge* that the reasons which he gives are adequate. We may also have to establish that he was not just guessing.

Thus, finding out whether Tommy knows something is quite unlike finding out whether he is 'sure' about something. If what we had to do in order to find out whether Tommy knew the date of the battle was merely to establish the fact that he was 'sure', or that he was in some unique state of mind, how could this be done? By asking him to pronounce on his state of mind? Would we then have to accept his report? We have already seen that even if he reported that he was sure, and we had no reason to disbelieve him, this would not guarantee the truth of what he was asserting: he could be sure and still be mistaken. But this is not the way we go about trying to decide whether someone knows something, such as whether Tommy knows how to mend a fuse, knows his way about Cardiff or knows that Great Britain is an island. We give him a broken fuse to mend and assess his performance; we ask him to take us from the City Hall to the railway station; we question him to see if he gives the right answer to the question 'Is Great Britain an island or a peninsula?' and we check his reasons and that he is not just guessing.

We are now in a position to review the assumptions which Professor Harrison claimed would have been taken for granted about the statement 'I know she will be late' (cf. pp. 103–4). Our reply may be summarised thus:

1. The statement 'I know she will be late' needs a context in order to be intelligible, such as where someone challenges my assertion 'She will be late', and I counter with 'I know . . .'

2. 'I know she will be late' is not a logically simple statement

which is true or false. It involves claiming that a proposition is true and that I am in a position to justify it, or that I have the right to assert it as a truth.

3. 'She will be late' could be true without my being in a position to assert it as a truth.

4. If I say 'I know she will be late', I am neither asserting two propositions, namely 'She will be late' and 'I know it' (i.e. a proposition about my mental attitude to the proposition, 'She will be late') nor am I asserting the one proposition 'I-know-that-she-will-be-late'. I am asserting the one proposition 'She will be late', and I am claiming that my assertion is true and justifiable.

5. The difference between my knowing one proposition and not knowing another does not lie in my 'mental attitude' to these propositions or in my 'state of mind'. The difference is that I am in a position to assert the one as a truth and not the other.

I conclude, then, that Austin was right in denying that the expression 'I know' describes either the occurrence of a mental act of 'knowing' or a state of mind which I am in. This conclusion holds even if, as I think we should, we abandon the parallelism between 'I know' and 'I promise'. We should add, however, that in order to deny that expressions such as 'I know' and 'he knows' describe states of mind, we need not say, as Austin appears to say, that they are not descriptive in *any* sense. It might well be contended, for example, that to say of someone that he has convincing reasons for asserting so-and-so is as descriptive as saying that he has red hair, though, of course, the procedures for verifying the two descriptions would vary. We should also concede that Austin's suggestions for equivalents for 'I know' may require some reformulation, namely 'I give others my word' and 'I give others my authority for saying that "S is P"'. It is not so much that I am giving others my authority for saying that 'S is P': I am asserting that 'S is P' and claiming that I could, if required, justify my assertion.

I have, therefore, rejected the first two versions of the doctrine mentioned at the start of the present chapter, namely the doctrine that knowing should be conceived of primarily in psychological terms. 'Knowing' is neither to be equated with 'being sure' nor with some special, unique state of mind. Before we consider the third version, namely that 'being sure', although not synonymous with 'knowing', is a necessary condition of knowing, we must discuss some issues concerned with the making and accepting of knowledge claims.

1. The fact that someone says 'I know' does not, of course, guarantee the truth of what he asserts. You can think that you know when you do not know. This is not to say that you can mis-identify some unique state of mind, mistake the state of mind of 'error' for the state of mind of 'knowledge'. It is to say that you can make claims when you are not entitled to make them, on the grounds, for example, that your conclusion has been invalidly drawn without your being aware of it. There are no claims which are self-justifying, either in the sense that the mere making of the claim provides its own guarantee, or in the sense that in no circumstances would a challenge be meaningful. The fact that in everyday life we frequently concede a knowledge claim without asking the claimant for his reasons or for his evidence, or without asking for a demonstration or proof, does not contradict this assertion: it does not mean that in no circumstances would a justification be called for. It does not invalidate the claim that the standard use of 'know' is that in which a person who says 'I know' is implying that he could justify himself if required to do so. Whether we ask for the justification before conceding the claim is not material. I may, for example, concede that my neighbour knows that it rained in Cardiff yesterday when I was in London: I may 'take his word for it'. But you might ask him why he asserted that it rained and demand a justification, if, for instance, you were cross-examining him in a law court.

2. Just as we may make claims when we are not entitled to make them, so it might well happen that we fail to make claims when we would be justified in making them. It is quite possible that I might be credited by other people with knowing something when I, through modesty, for example, might shrink from making a knowledge claim. This applies equally to 'knowing how' and 'knowing that'. Thus, the boy at school who stands in awe of mathematics might be told by his teacher who has watched his performance, and who is competent to assess it, that he knows how to solve quadratic equations. This might come as a shock or a revelation to the boy who hitherto, through modesty or timidity, has been reluctant to make so bold a claim and who, when asked whether he knows how to solve quadratic equations, has contented himself with tentative remarks such as 'I think I know how to do them', or perhaps has even denied that he knows how to do them. Or again, the over-scrupulous historian may be reluctant or

hesitant to say that he knows that Edward I was a spendthrift, even though his professional colleagues are prepared to concede that he has established it.

3. I have said that for someone to say 'Tommy knows that Great Britain is an island' is not a simple true-or-false statement about Tommy's state of mind or mental attitude towards a proposition, but that it is, rather, the conceding of Tommy's claim that he is right and right for the right reasons. This conceding of his claim is based on an assessment of what he says and his reasons for saying it. Just as Tommy may make claims to which he is not entitled, so we may concede that Tommy knows when we have no right to do so. Our assessments of his 'knowings' are as fallible as our assessments of his intelligence or his generosity. Just as Tommy may have to withdraw a claim to know something, so we may have to withdraw our acceptance of his claim, for example because of a deeper inquiry into his reasons (he was guessing after all, though we did not suspect it at the time) or new considerations may now have arisen of which we were unaware at the time (Edward I had, in fact, made substantial savings which had escaped our notice). Thus, saying of someone 'He knows so-and-so' is just as corrigible as someone saying 'I know' of himself. To those philosophers who think of statements of the form 'I know . . .' and 'he knows . . .' as statements of 'objective facts' about people, statements which are either true or false in a clear-cut way comparable with statements of the form 'He was born at sea', this conclusion will, no doubt, prove unacceptable. But we are quite familiar with the idea that what is accepted as knowledge today may have to be revised tomorrow: the history of man's aspirations to knowledge is full of such revisions. We are also familiar with other situations where we are called upon to make judgements or assessments of some-one's behaviour which are different from simple 'discoveries of facts', which are not 'right-once-and-for-all' statements of facts, for instance judging someone to be wiser now than he was as a young man, judging that he is wittier than his colleagues, judging that he is better behaved at parties than he used to be, etc. We do not regard assessments of this kind as being either infallible or irrevocable, nor, of course, do we assume that they are never sound. Equally, examiners have to assess whether someone knows how to drive a car, or whether someone knows that a gas will expand if heated. Their assessments have sometimes to be revised.

4. We do not always insist on the same standards of rigour in conceding knowledge claims. We try not to be more pedantic than the occasion demands. If, however, someone said that he knew some geometrical truth, it would be appropriate, especially in the context of an examination, to ask for a demonstration. We take several factors into consideration, for example the standing of the claimant—whether he is a recognised authority on the matter in question, whether he is generally reliable on questions of fact or whether he has a reputation for jumping to conclusions. It also makes a good deal of difference whether the matters which the claimant says he knows are already familiar or well established, as, for example, the date of the Battle of Hastings or the atomic weight of tin. We are naturally more pressing if the claimant comes up with something new, for instance if he says that he knows that there is another planet whose existence has hitherto not been suspected, or if he says that he knows that the St Matthew Passion hitherto credited to Bach was written by Telemann. We should not conclude from this variation in standards that we are irresponsible either in making knowledge claims or in conceding them. Standards of rigour which are appropriate in an academic seminar may well be inappropriate in the market place or playground. Nor should we accuse the public of using the word 'knowledge' loosely if sometimes it concedes knowledge claims without rigorous scrutiny: the public is simply being sensible.

5. The question may be asked, 'Who is to decide whether someone knows that so-and-so is the case?' or 'Who is to decide whether someone knows how to solve quadratic equations?' There are, I think, three errors which have to be avoided in this connection. The first error is that of assuming that the claimant is himself the best judge of whether he knows something or not. Indeed, if 'knowing' was an experience, a mental act or an unique mental state, there might be a strong case for saying that the decision should be left to the claimant. But since 'knowing' is not in any sense an experience, this answer is not available to us. It would be tantamount to saying that the person who makes a claim is the person who should set the criteria for assessing its validity and also decide whether in an individual case the criteria had been satisfied. But this would make nonsense of the notion of a 'claim'. Claims are things which we make to *other* people, not to ourselves, and the criteria for assessing their validity must be inter-personal or public. The person who says that he knows

something is always liable to be challenged to substantiate his claim, either by offering evidence in its support or by displaying the arguments for the conclusion he has arrived at, etc. The evidence which he offers, or the arguments which he discloses, are subject to public scrutiny. To say that the claimant is not in the best position to concede his own claims is not, however, to say that I cannot assess my own claims by operating with agreed public criteria of logical validity, etc. What is ruled out is that I can assess my own claims by operating with criteria set up by myself, either in disregard or in defiance of publicly agreed standards. I can, of course, check my own syllogisms, but only by operating with agreed rules of inference. Whereas we do not require the sanction of others in order to say that we *believe* so-and-so (though the question whether or not the belief is a rational or reasonable one *is* open to public scrutiny), nor do we need the sanction of others to say that we have a headache, we need to satisfy common criteria if we wish our knowledge claims to be accepted, just as we have to satisfy agreed grammatical rules if we wish to communicate with others.

The second error to be avoided is that of assuming that there is a criterion available for assessing the validity of any knowledge claim made in any sphere, as if someone who claimed to know a historical truth and someone who claimed to know a mathematical truth had to satisfy some common criterion or criteria in precisely the same way. Clearly the method of assessing a knowledge claim will vary from one subject-matter to another. In the case of a mathematical claim, for instance, we would ask for a rigorous deductive proof; in the case of a historical claim we would ask for a no less rigorous, though non-deductive, demonstration that the evidence justified the conclusion; in the case of a claim made in an experimental subject such as chemistry, we would scrutinise the observations and the experiments on which the claim was based. There is no analogue to the British Standard Yard which can be used to assess all knowledge claims.

The third error to be avoided is that of assuming that it is, as it were, open to any member of the public indiscriminately to assess the validity of any knowledge claim made in any sphere. This is, of course, absurd. The only people who can be in a position to judge whether I know how to solve quadratic equations are those who know how to solve them themselves. The layman is not in a position to assess the claim made by the physician that he knows that the patient is suffering from German measles, nor can he assess the physicist's claim that he knows that there is another elementary particle in addition to those already accounted for.

We can now consider the third version of the doctrine that knowing is to conceived of in psychological terms. This is the view that 'being sure' is a necessary condition of knowing. If we are not to *equate* 'knowing' with 'being sure' or with being in a special state of mind, is there a case for saying that a person cannot be credited with knowing something unless he is sure of what he asserts? Or, is 'being sure' just an accidental accompaniment of knowing, or even, perhaps, is it irrelevant to knowing?

The view that 'being sure' is a necessary condition of knowing has had many adherents. Thus, Professor A. J. Ayer, who argues against the *equating* of 'knowing' with 'being in a special mental state', asserts that 'being sure' is one of the necessary and sufficient conditions of knowledge, the others being that what one is said to know is true and that one has the right to be sure (*The Problem of Knowledge* (Penguin Books, 1956) pp. 31 ff). In much the same vein, Professor Malcolm says 'Being confident is a necessary condition for knowing' ('Knowledge and Belief', *Mind*, Vol. 51 (1952), reprinted in Phillips Griffiths (ed.), *Knowledge and Belief* (Oxford University Press, 1967) p. 70).

'Being sure' is a very elusive concept. Some writers explicitly refer to it as 'feeling sure', as if this was the description of some experience which necessarily accompanies knowing. It is not clear, I think, whether Professor Malcolm's use of 'being confident' is intended thus. But other writers clearly wish to distinguish between 'being sure' and 'feeling sure'. Professor Ayer, for example (*op. cit.*, pp. 16–17), after speaking of 'being sure', goes on to speak of 'to be convinced of something', as if this was synonymous with 'being sure'. But he then adds that 'though to be convinced of something is, in a sense, to be in a particular state of mind, it does not seem to consist in any special mental occurrence. It is rather a matter of accepting the fact in question and of not being at all disposed to doubt it than of contemplating it with a conscious feeling of conviction.' He adds, further, that though such feelings of conviction exist, 'it is not certain that to have a feeling of conviction is even a sufficient condition for being sure'. He thus appears to be distinguishing between 'being sure' and 'feeling sure'.

What, then, is 'being sure' if it is different from 'feeling sure'? In what sense can it be described as a positive state of mind which, it is alleged, is a necessary accompaniment or condition of knowing? Is there such a state of mind which also admits of degrees? Professor Ayer distinguishes between 'being unsure', 'being sure', 'being quite sure' and 'being altogether sure'. Are we to regard these as different states of mind or as different degrees of intensity in one and the same state of mind? Further, are we to regard 'being unsure' as a positive state of mind?

I think that Professor Ayer himself has given the answers to these questions when he says that 'to be convinced . . . is not being at all disposed to doubt' (*op. cit.*, pp. 16–17). In other words, 'being sure', which appears at first sight to indicate some positive, introspectible state of mind which someone must be in, if he is knowing, turns out to be the *absence* of something, namely the *absence* of doubt. And, indeed, this is what it is. The passage from 'opinion' to 'being inclined to believe' to 'believing' to 'believing firmly', etc., does not consist in an increase in intensity in some positive feeling: one proceeds along the route from opinion to conviction by the gradual elimination of doubt. Doubt, itself, in the sense of 'being disinclined to believe' (as opposed to denying that *p* is true) is, I would argue, wrongly described as a 'positive feeling' or 'positive state of mind'.

The doctrine that 'being sure is a condition of knowing' has, then, to be reformulated to 'knowing is incompatible with doubting'. This might sound as if what is being said is that there is some fundamental opposition between two mental states, that of doubting and that of knowing, as if what is being said is that a person cannot be in both mental states at one and the same time. But this is clearly not what is intended. What is intended becomes clear when we examine the argument which is usually offered in support of the contention that 'being sure' is a condition of knowing. The argument is that it would be self-contradictory to *say* of oneself that one knew that such-and-such a statement was true, but that one was not altogether sure of it (cf. Ayer, *op. cit.*, p. 16). Thus, 'being sure is a condition of knowing' becomes 'One should not assert that *p* is true and that one is prepared to justify it if one has any doubts either about the truth of *p* or the validity of one's justification'. In other words, it is a condition for making knowledge claims.

It is instructive to compare the account given by Professor Ayer with that given by Professor Malcolm. The remark which was quoted from Malcolm, namely 'Being confident is a necessary condition for knowing', has to be interpreted in the light of what precedes it. Earlier in the same paragraph Malcolm says 'Whether we would say that you knew, depends in part on how *confident* you were' and 'If you lack confidence that *p* is true then others do not say that you know that *p* is true, even though *they* know that *p* is true'. It is clear from this that what Malcolm intends by 'being confident is a necessary condition for knowing' is 'a condition for conceding a knowledge claim is that the claimant should make his claim confidently'. Ayer seems to be concerned with when one should make knowledge claims and Malcolm with when one should concede them.

There are many reasons for rejecting these attempts to make 'being sure' a necessary condition for knowing. In the first place, it is not always possible to tell whether someone is confident in making a claim or not: such claims may be written as well as spoken, and there may be no indication of the degree of confidence of the writer. Nevertheless, if what he asserts is true, and we are satisfied that his reasons for asserting it are adequate, we show no compunction in crediting him with knowledge. If, however, it is a necessary condition that the person should be sure, then there could be no sense in crediting him with knowing something unless this condition was seen to be satisfied. We can, and do, grant someone the status of knowing something *in absentia*. The point could also be put by saying that we could not sensibly be required to prove that someone did not doubt before accepting positive evidence for knowledge, nor, when offering conclusive reasons for my claim, need I add, 'and I don't doubt it'.

In the second place, as we saw earlier, it might well happen that others would be prepared to credit someone with knowledge even if he was reluctant to claim knowledge himself. A boy at school, for example, when asked by his teacher whether he knows what the genitive plural of *mensa* is, might be reluctant or hesitant to say that he knew. If, however, he gave the right answer, and the teacher, after satisfying himself that the boy knew what nouns were, what the rules were for the declension of first declension latin nouns, etc., and after trying him out on other examples was satisfied that he was not guessing, the teacher might well tell the boy that of course he knew what the genitive plural of *mensa* is, and advise him not to be so cautious in future. That is, a man may well be credited by others with knowing something, even if he himself is not prepared to go further than saying 'I think I know'. There is no self-contradiction in saying 'He does in fact know, though he only thinks he knows', any more than there is in saying 'He thinks he knows, but in fact he does not know'. Thus, although it might seem odd in some contexts for someone to say that he knew, and yet to admit to some doubts, it is not a logical oddity in the sense of a self-contradiction. His doubts would not prevent him knowing. It is of interest to notice that there is considerable divergence in the uses of 'know' and 'believe' in this connection. Thus, while it makes sense to say 'He does in fact know how to do so-and-so, or know that so-and-so, although he only thinks he knows', it is nonsense to say 'He does in fact believe so-and-so, although he only thinks he believes'.

The irrelevance of 'being sure' is particularly noticeable in the case of 'knowing how'. In assessing whether someone knows how to tie a bow tie, we are not interested in his state of mind, whether he is sure or not: we are interested only in his performance. Very often, we find, the best drivers are those who retain a healthy modesty about their abilities.

Finally, the realisation of the dispositional nature of knowledge, which was emphasised in earlier chapters, points to the irrelevance of psychological factors such as 'being sure' or 'being confident'. Since to say of someone that he knows how to swim or that he knows that Great Britain is an island is not to talk about what he is doing now, and since someone may know something even when he is not attending to it, this shows that the relevance of 'being sure', if it is ever relevant, is not to 'knowing that p is true', but to '*saying* that one knows . . . .'.

We have already seen that 'being sure' is not even a necessary condition of '*saying* that one knows' or of conceding that someone knows. Not only would it be absurd in practice to recommend that no one should be credited with knowing anything unless it was established that he was sure: the alleged logical self-contradiction in saying 'He knows, though he is not sure', or 'He knows, though he only thinks he knows', is illusory.

We must, therefore, agree with Professor Woozley when he says 'The tendency to psychologize knowing . . . dies hard', and agree further with his diagnosis that 'a part cause of that may be in the continuance of this mistake. It is the mistake of thinking that a man cannot know something unless he is sure of it'. ('Knowing and not Knowing', *Proceedings of the Aristotelian Society*, Vol. 53

(1952–3) p. 151, reprinted in Phillips Griffiths (ed.), *Knowledge and Belief* (Oxford University Press, 1967) p. 82.)

In concluding this chapter, I should like to consider again the problem of the 'reflexiveness' of knowledge, which was mentioned in Chapter 6, namely the claim made by some philosophers that we cannot know without knowing that we know. We noticed that this contention had the unwelcome result of introducing an infinite regress, in that if I know that I know, by the same argument it follows that I must know that I know that I know, and so on.

We can now see, I think, that the difficulty arises only because of the error of regarding 'knowing' either as a mental act or as a mental state. Thus, on the first alternative, it might be superficially plausible to say that if I perform the act of knowing, it is not possible for me not to know (not to be aware of the fact) that I am performing the act of knowing. But the knowing that I am performing the act of knowing is itself an act of knowing, which I cannot perform without knowing that I am performing it, etc. If one act of knowing occurs, there must be another to follow it, *ad infinitum*. On the second alternative, it might seem plausible to say that I cannot be in the mental state of knowing unless I know (in the active sense of 'know') that I am in that state, any more than I cannot be hungry without knowing that I am hungry. The introduction of the active sense of 'know' will, of course, start off a regress.

If, however, the conclusions of this and the preceding chapters are correct, it follows that the question 'Do I know that I know?' or 'How do I know that I know?' has to be reformulated. The problem is not that of being able to identify some experience of knowing when it occurs, nor of being able to identify some peculiar state of mind which one is in. 'Am I knowing or am I in error?' is not a question which can be answered by an inspection of one's state of mind, by asking oneself whether one feels confident or sure, or by catching oneself doing an act of knowing. Questions such as 'Do I know how to tie a bow tie?', 'Do I know what the capital of Mexico is?', 'Do I know that if all men are wise and Tommy is a man, therefore Tommy is wise?' are answered, for example, by trying my hand at tying a bow tie, by consulting a reference book, by checking the validity of my argument. The question 'Do I know . . . ?' is no different in this respect from the question 'Does he know . . . ?' If we wish to discover whether someone knows how to tie a bow tie, we do not ask him whether he has performed a cognitive act, nor do we ask him to examine his state of mind and report on it. We study his performance or we check his conclusions and the way he got to them. Otherwise only I could know if I knew, and I would have to take your word for it if you said that you knew. The position with knowledge is quite different from that which holds in the case of belief, where a person can, by means of self-examination, tell whether he believes something. The difference is due to the fact that knowing necessarily involves being right and belief does not. You cannot tell by how you feel whether Paris is the capital of France or of Germany. The test of being right is not my state of mind, but what the external facts are. Once we stop thinking of knowing as a mental act or as a mental state, the reflexive bogey vanishes.

9 Knowledge and Belief

During the course of this book I have emphasised the striking contrast between some of the assumptions about knowledge which we make in everyday life and some of the things which many philosophers say when they theorise about knowledge. Thus, I have defended our widespread practice of being prepared to consider, and sometimes to concede, knowledge claims in a variety of subjects, such as history, botany, chemistry, etc., as well as in everyday circumstances: this was in opposition to the philosophical theory that the possibility of achieving knowledge is, in principle, restricted to such disciplines as logic and mathematics. I could find no good reason why we should not, in appropriate situations, continue to say that we knew that Sir Francis Drake was buried at sea, that oak trees shed their leaves in winter, that a gas will expand if heated, that the coal bucket is empty. In brief, we can claim knowledge of contingent as well as of necessary truths. A corollary of this conclusion was that propositions should not be classified as those which are inherently or intrinsically 'knowable' and those which are inherently or intrinsically 'believable'. I defended also the commonly held view that knowledge cannot be distinguished from belief simply by an examination of one's state of mind.

Throughout this discussion there has been an implicit, and sometimes an explicit, reference to a contrast between knowledge and belief, but no direct consideration has been given to the precise nature of the contrast. This is the theme of the present chapter.

The one point on which there is general agreement is that what we know can only be true, whereas what we believe may be true and may be false. I have previously described this as the minimal interpretation of the dictum that knowledge cannot be mistaken (Chapter 3). This interpretation implies no more than the fact that the disjunction 'either true or false' does not apply to what we know but does apply to what we believe.

It must not, however, be assumed that the acceptance of the minimal interpretation of this dictum commits us to any particular view concerning the relation of knowledge to belief: it is, indeed, compatible with two radically different views. It might, for instance, suggest that knowledge and belief are wholly opposed to each other, in the sense that it is impossible to define one in terms of the other, and particularly that knowledge cannot be regarded as a specific variety of belief. But although it is compatible with this position, it does not imply it: it also leaves open the possibility that knowledge is a type of belief. The acceptance of the dictum would, indeed, prevent us from identifying knowledge with belief which is false, but the dictum would be satisfied if we identified knowledge with belief which is true. Its only stipulation is that in no circumstances would it be correct to say that what someone knows is false.

It would not, indeed, suffice simply to say that knowledge is equivalent to 'true belief', since there are other implications in the notion of knowledge which this attempted identification would neglect. Thus, before we are prepared to credit someone with knowing something, we need to be assured not only that the proposition which he claims to be true *is* true, but that he has not arrived at it just 'by accident', or as the result of an invalid argument, etc. If, for example, I say that I know that the atomic weight of tin is so-and-so, my hearer will seek to be assured that I am not just guessing or repeating, parrot-fashion, what I have heard, before he will be prepared to concede that I know it. Any attempt to define knowledge in terms of belief must, therefore, take these considerations into account: 'knowledge is true belief' will have to be qualified in such terms as, 'knowledge is true, justified belief'. If, then, someone believes that a proposition is true and the proposition *is* true, and if he is able to substantiate it by providing a demonstration or proof, there is no reason, on this view, why we should not say that he *knows* that the proposition is true.

My initial point needs, I think, to be emphasised in view of the over-hasty conclusions which have sometimes been drawn in this connection. It is that the acceptance of the minimal interpretation of the dictum 'knowledge cannot be mistaken' does not in itself commit us either to the view that knowledge and belief must be totally opposed to each other or to the contrary view that knowledge can be defined as a specific variety of belief. Clearly, some further considerations must be advanced to justify a choice between these two rival positions. The issue which faces us is what sort of contrast between knowledge and belief is required by our everyday use of the concept of knowledge. Philosophical theories which are advanced to explain the relation between them will have to be evaluated in the light of this criterion.

Although the minimal interpretation of the dictum that knowledge cannot be mistaken is neutral between rival theories, yet the extension of the dictum to mean 'knowledge must be infallible' (which was discussed in Chapters 3 and 4) clearly commits us to the view that knowledge and belief are radically different. If to say that someone knows p is incompatible with even the theoretical possibility of being mistaken, then in no circumstances would it be possible to define knowledge in terms of belief, however qualified. This would be so because the possibility of being mistaken is never ruled out when we say that someone believes p. Thus, even if a belief were true, and could be justified, it would necessarily fall short of the conditions for knowledge, if knowledge is described as 'infallible'.

We have already considered and rejected one version of the doctrine that knowledge and belief are wholly opposed to each other, namely the Platonic view of the difference between knowledge and belief (Chapter 4). This view, based largely on the premiss that knowledge must be infallible, was distinctive not only in insisting that knowing and believing are quite different 'powers' or 'faculties', but in insisting further that they are concerned with quite different 'objects'. Plato, indeed, seems to have thought that knowledge and belief could not be differentiated unless they could be shown to be concerned with separate objects. Thus, the objects of knowledge were said to be Forms or Universals, and the objects of belief, Particulars. This view was rejected for two main reasons. It was contended that the extension of the dictum, 'knowledge cannot be mistaken' to mean 'knowledge must be infallible' was unjustified, and Plato's arguments for crediting knowledge and belief with different objects were rejected on their own merits as well as being shown to be

inconsistent with our common practice of assuming that knowledge and belief are concerned with the same things.

It would, however, be hazardous to conclude from the failure of
this attempt to distinguish radically between knowledge and
belief, that they can be assimilated. Though they may not have
separate objects, they may well be different on other grounds. One
contemporary view which regards knowing and believing as
radically different, but without involving a difference of objects, is
forcibly expressed by Prichard, largely following Cook Wilson, in
Knowledge and Perception (Oxford: The Clarendon Press, 1950),
reprinted in part in Phillips Griffiths (ed.), *Knowledge and Belief*
(Oxford University Press, 1967) pp. 60–8). According to
Prichard, knowing is 'absolutely different' from believing or being
convinced. The difference is described as being a difference 'in
kind' and not simply a difference 'in degree'. A difference 'in kind'
is specified as the sort of difference which there is between
'desiring' and 'feeling', or between a red colour and a blue colour.
It is not to be confused with the difference which there is between
a species and a genus, such as between a red colour and a colour.
Thus, to know is not to have a special kind of belief which is
different from other kinds of belief, and 'no improvement in a
belief . . . will convert it into knowledge'. Nor is the difference
comparable to that of being two species of a common genus: for
example, they are not both species of the genus 'thinking', of
which knowing is the better kind and belief the worse. The only
connection which Prichard allows between them is '(a) that
believing presupposes knowing, though, of course, knowing something other than what we believe, and (b) that believing is a stage
we sometimes reach in the endeavour to attain knowledge'
(Prichard, *op. cit.*, pp. 87–8; Griffiths, *op. cit.*, p. 62).

Some of Prichard's contentions are, in my view, acceptable; I
shall myself argue in favour of his conclusion that to know is not to
have a special kind of belief which is different from other kinds of
belief. But his description of the difference between knowledge
and belief is unacceptable for several reasons. The most important consideration is that Prichard is committed to the view that
'knowing' is some sort of 'experience' or 'mental state', and the
difference 'in kind' to which he refers is said to be a difference
between two incompatible 'states or conditions of mind', similar,
as he says, to the difference between desiring and feeling. He
further contends that 'when we know something, we either do or

can directly know that we are knowing it, and when we believe something we know or can know that we are believing and not knowing it' (Prichard, *op. cit.*, p. 96; Griffiths, *op. cit.*, p. 66). We have, however, (Chapters 7 and 8) rejected both the view that knowing can be described as an occurrence or experience and the view that knowing is some sort of mental state or condition. It followed from this rejection that knowing was not self-certifying, in the sense that when we know something we cannot help knowing that we know it. The verb 'to know', it was argued, is not a 'doing' verb: it does not denote an act or activity, nor does it denote some unique, infallible state of mind, nor the condition of 'being sure'. If these conclusions are acceptable, it follows that it is just as unprofitable to try to draw a radical distinction between knowledge and belief in terms of a distinction between two incompatible 'states of mind' as it proved unprofitable to distinguish them in terms of their being concerned with entirely different objects.

Further, the reason which Prichard actually gives for the distinction which he draws is too vague to be helpful. The difference between knowledge and belief, he says, can be seen immediately by considering that 'we should only say that we know something when we are certain of it, and conversely, and that in the end we have to allow that the meaning of the terms is identical: whereas, on the other hand, when we believe something we are uncertain of it' (Prichard, *op. cit.*, p. 88; Griffiths, *op. cit.*, pp. 62–3). The vagueness is in the phrase 'we are certain'. This could be interpreted as meaning that when we say that we know something we do so only when what we have claimed to know has been established as being true, whereas when we say that we believe something we do so only when what we believe to be true is still disputable. But this interpretation would not entail a difference 'in kind' between two mental states, but only a difference in the contexts in which 'I know' and 'I believe' are used. If, however, it is taken to mean that when we say that we know something, *we* are certain of what we assert, this can only mean either (a) that we are convinced or sure—an interpretation which Prichard would reject since he denies that a difference of degree of confidence distinguishes knowing from believing—or (b) that we should say that we know something only when we know it, which is unchallengeable but uninformative. In any case, the fact that *we* are 'certain' would not guarantee that we are right.

The description of the difference between knowledge and belief as a difference 'in kind' rather than 'in degree' must itself be questioned. Indeed, it may well be that one of the chief reasons why the connection between knowledge and belief has proved to be such an intractable problem is because of the introduction of this distinction. Part of the trouble arises, I think, because of the tendency to regard knowledge and belief, in Prichard's terms, as 'absolutely different', or, as is sometimes said, as 'opposites'. But this is much too simple a view. To the question 'What is the opposite of knowledge?' there can be more than one answer, depending on which feature of knowledge is being emphasised. If we are thinking of knowledge in terms of the possession of information, then it would be intelligible to say that the opposite of knowledge is ignorance. If, however, our interest is in the fact that it is a necessary feature of knowledge that what is known is true, the opposite of knowledge might be said to be error, a necessary feature of which is that it is mistaken. Again, if we are concentrating on the aspect of knowledge where to say that someone knows something is to say that he has conclusive reasons for what he asserts to be true, or is able to demonstrate its truth, then the opposite of knowledge might appear to be belief, where there is not the same implication that the person who says that he believes is in a position to offer conclusive reasons or proof. At other times, the opposite of knowing might be said to be 'guessing', for example, if we are assured that someone had hit on the right answer to a question simply by chance, we might say 'You don't know the answer, you are just guessing'. But not one of these, ignorance, error, belief or guessing, is the 'real opposite' of knowledge.

It would, indeed, be strange if knowledge and belief should turn out to be totally dissimilar, or 'absolutely different'. Whereas it is obvious that the terms 'knowledge' and 'belief' are not synonymous or interchangeable, it is also clear that they are related to each other in certain ways. The similarities between them might well not be such as to justify the defining of knowledge in terms of belief, but equally they might rule out the attempt to describe the difference between them as one of 'kind rather than degree'. Whereas they are not co-terminous, since there is no analogue in the case of belief for 'knowing how' and no analogue in the case of knowledge for 'believing in', yet they operate, to some extent, as it were in the same territory. They are both 'intellectual' dispositions, and both are connected, though in a different way, with the notion of truth. We may compare, in this respect, the connection between the notions of 'choice' and 'decision'. Though they are not synonymous, they are yet related to each other: they operate, broadly, in the same territory. They are not wholly unrelated to each other in the way in which choice, for example, is wholly unrelated to the notion of depression. But how could one answer the question 'Do choice and decision differ in kind or only in degree?' Thus, the mere fact that knowledge and belief are used in the same general context shows that they are not wholly unrelated; it is significant, for example, to say 'Whereas he only believes that Paris is the capital of France, I know that it is'. But equally, the fact that they have to some extent a common field of operation does not entail that they are inter-definable, since there is, as in the above example, some kind of contrast between them. I am suggesting, therefore, that the attempt to understand the differences between knowledge and belief in terms of a difference in kind or a difference in degree can only result in confusion. What we should do is to mark the similarities and the differences between them, and not force upon them a distinction which is here totally inapplicable, though applicable, possibly, in other contexts.

If, then, we reject the view that knowledge and belief are totally opposed to each other, either in the Platonic version which involves a radical difference in their objects, or in Prichard's version, where knowledge and belief are regarded as states of mind which differ in kind, are we committed to the view that knowledge can be defined in terms of belief, as, for example, true, justified belief?

There seem to be two main arguments which are commonly advanced in support of the view that knowledge should be so defined. The first is a negative type of argument, based on the rejection of the thesis that knowledge and belief are concerned with entirely different objects. If, then, they are concerned with the same subject-matter, if they have the same 'objects', there is no reason, it is concluded, why knowledge should not be subsumed under belief. I have already suggested that it would be hazardous to conclude that knowledge and belief could be assimilated simply because of the failure of the attempt to accord them separate objects: there might well be other compelling reasons against such an assimilation. One contemporary version of this argument is that since the distinction between knowledge and belief cannot be explained in terms of saying that knowledge is concerned with necessary truths and belief with contingent propositions, there cannot be a radical difference between them. But, in fact, although it may be correct, in a given situation, to say that I know that the coal bucket is empty (a proposition which is only contingently true) and correct to say that you believe it, this does not, in itself, justify the conclusion that knowledge is a variety of belief, even if the qualifications are added that the proposition which is believed is true and is justified. It no more follows that knowledge is a variety of belief from the fact that I can believe what you know than it follows that hope is a variety of fear, or *vice-versa*, from the fact that I can hope what you fear.

The second argument is based on the premiss that knowledge must at least *involve* belief. This is taken to provide the first 'condition' for knowledge, namely that the person who knows *p* must believe *p*. Further conditions are then added, such as that the proposition is true and that the person who believes it is justified in believing it. The success of the suggested assimilation of knowledge to true, justified belief is thus entirely dependent on the truth of the initial premiss that knowing implies believing. How is this vital premiss established? It is derived from the fact that it would be inconsistent for someone to say that he knew so-and-so but that he did not believe it. From this alleged incongruity it is inferred that, therefore, if someone knows so-and-so, he must also believe it. There is, indeed, an air of paradox about the question 'Must a man believe what he knows?' It suggests that if we answer in the negative, i.e. if we say that a man who knows something does not believe it, we are then committed to saying that if someone knows something, then he disbelieves what he knows, which would, of course, be nonsense. But the question leads to this absurdity only if it is presupposed that when someone knows something, he must *either* believe *or* disbelieve what he knows. The desired answer, that a man must believe what he knows, follows only because it is presupposed by the terms of the question.

We get quite a different result if we say that when someone knows something, he *neither* believes *nor* disbelieves what he knows. It would, indeed, be incongruous for someone to say that he knew something but disbelieved it, but it would *not* follow from this incongruity that he therefore had to believe it. It would, in fact, be equally incongruous to say that 'knowing *p*' *meant* 'believing *p*' (with further qualifications about the truth of *p* and the ability to justify it) or to say that when someone knew *p*, in addition to knowing it he *also* believed it. Thus, the plausibility of the view that knowledge involves belief rests entirely on the unwarranted assumption that if someone knows something, he *must either* believe *or* disbelieve what he knows.

The question 'Does a man who knows something also believe it?' is misleading in two further ways. In the first place, it may suggest that the issue to be decided is whether there is an equation between two states of mind. Our rejection of the view that knowledge is a state of mind, however, rules out this suggestion. In the second place, it may suggest that the problem is that of identifying the extra ingredients which will transform belief into knowledge. Hence the familiar attempts to introduce such extras as 'being sure' or 'being certain' or 'conviction' which will, as it were, give belief the leg up to convert it into knowledge. Professor Gettier has, I think, shown the impossibility of such attempts to state the extra 'conditions' for converting belief into knowledge in his paper 'Is Justified True Belief Knowledge?' (*Analysis*, Vol. 23 (1963) 121–3, reprinted in Phillips Griffiths (ed.), *Knowledge and Belief* (Oxford University Press, 1967), pp. 144–6). There have been many ingenious attempts to restate the extra conditions for knowledge in such a way as to avoid Gettier's criticisms, but, in my view, all such attempts fail because the initial step of defining knowledge as a form of belief is mistaken. The question, then, is not that of trying to decide what extra one has to do in addition to believing something in order to know it, nor of deciding between those beliefs which constitute knowledge and those which do not: it is the question of marking the difference between the situation where someone affirms that he believes so-and-so and the situation where he claims to know that so-and-so is the case. Nor, of course, is it the question of trying to decide at what point in the scale of 'sureness' one crosses the frontier between believing and knowing, for example when 'being sure' becomes 'being absolutely sure' or 'being certain'. Psychological notions, such as 'being sure' or 'being certain' or 'being confident', as we have seen earlier, are irrelevant to knowledge but relevant to belief.

The question whether or not knowing implies believing cannot, I think, conclusively be settled simply by an examination of linguistic fashions. Such considerations suggest that there is a contrast between knowledge and belief rather than that knowledge can be reduced to belief, but they are not decisive. Thus it makes sense to ask whether someone knows or merely believes that Paris is the capital of France, which suggests that they should be contrasted rather than assimilated. More decisive, perhaps, is what we would say in a situation such as the following. If someone said that he believed that brandy had beneficial effects, he would say so because he did not know it to be true. If, then, it was conclusively established that brandy had the beneficial effects in question, and he was aware of and understood the reasons, he would not continue to say that he believed it: he would say that he *knew* it. Nor would he be satisfied if he were told that where formerly he just believed it, he was now in the position of holding a belief which was true and justified: he would insist that he *knew* it. He would not say that now he knew it in addition to believing it: 'I believe' (however qualified) would have to *give way to* 'I know'.

My contention that the initial step of regarding knowledge as a form of belief is mistaken is, I think, best defended not merely by considering the different contextual requirements of 'I know' and 'I believe' but by considering also the different ways in which knowledge and belief are related to other key concepts.

Both the person who says 'I know that lead is malleable' and the person who says 'I believe that lead is malleable' are prepared to assert the categorical proposition 'Lead is malleable'. But the critical point of difference is that the person who says 'I know' is claiming both that the proposition which he asserts to be true *is* true and that he can demonstrate or justify its truth in a way which will satisfy publicly agreed criteria. On the other hand, the person who says 'I believe' is not, in the same way, claiming that he is right and that he can substantiate his claim. To say 'I believe' is to make an affirmation; to say 'I know' is to make a claim: the former is provisional, the latter is unreserved. Thus, if someone says 'I know', he is always liable to be asked 'How do you know?', i.e. he is liable to be asked for his justification of his claim. If the justification is not forthcoming, or is deemed to be unacceptable (for instance, if it is shown to be based on an invalid argument), the questioner will refuse to concede the claim, and may well ask the claimant to withdraw it. On the other hand, if someone says 'I believe', the appropriate rejoinder is not 'How do you believe it?' but rather 'Why do you believe it?'

It would, however, be a gross oversimplification to suggest that the request for reasons is appropriate in the case of a knowledge claim but inappropriate where someone says 'I believe'. One may, indeed, ask for reasons in the case of belief. But the request for reasons is made with a view to deciding whether the belief is a 'reasonable' one for the believer to hold in the light of the reasons which he offers. We ask for a justification in the case of knowledge, but not in order to be able to pronounce on the 'reasonableness' of the claim: in no circumstances would we say, for instance, 'Yes, I agree that it is reasonable for you to know so-and-so'. Again in contrast with the situation in knowledge claims, if the reasons advanced for holding a belief turn out to be unacceptable, we do not refuse to accept that the person believes it: there is no question of asking him to withdraw his statement that he believes it now (unless, of course, we are suspicious of his sincerity). We might, indeed, say that he 'ought not to believe it', because of the poverty of his reasons, but there would be no sense in telling someone whose knowledge claim is rejected that he 'ought not to know it'. As Austin remarks in 'Other Minds' (reprinted in *Philosophical Papers*, 2nd ed. (Oxford University Press, 1970), p. 78), we might, indeed, say that he ought not to *say* that he knew it, but we would not correspondingly say 'You ought not to say you believe it'. In Austin's words, 'You ought *to say* you believe it, if you do believe it, however poor the evidence' (footnote, p. 78).

The refusal to concede a knowledge claim is, therefore, tantamount to saying that the person who says he knows does not, in fact, know. A refusal to accept that someone has good reasons for holding a certain belief is not tantamount to saying that he does not believe what he says he believes. If we were dissatisfied with a person's reasons, we might try to persuade him to give up his beliefs: there could be no situation in which one might try to persuade someone to change his knowledge, or to give up what he knows.

We saw that whereas a belief could be described as 'reasonable', knowledge could not. Belief may be subject to such qualifications as 'rational', 'irrational' or 'non-rational', but such qualifications make no sense if applied to knowledge. Thus, someone may believe something simply because he wants it to be true: belief may be 'caused' by irrational factors such as hope, desire or fear, as well as being based on reasons. Or again, someone may believe something, in the sense that he takes something for granted, without having any conscious reasons for his belief: we can believe something in a habitual way. But in no circumstances would it be apt to say that someone knew something 'irrationally', or that he knew something 'merely from habit'.

The difference between knowledge and belief is sometimes drawn in terms of saying that knowledge is 'objective' and belief is 'subjective'. But this distinction can be interpreted in several ways. Thus, on the Platonic view, 'objective' corresponds to 'the real' and 'subjective' to 'the semi-real'. In contemporary terms, this is the distinction between 'facts' as entities or bits of reality and propositions as bits of language, or as inferior entities which sentences mean. Or again, it is said that knowledge is of 'reality itself' and belief is of a 'picture of reality'. But the difference between someone who knows that the Battle of Waterloo was fought in 1815 and someone who merely believes it is not to be explained as a difference between the one being in direct contact with a chunk of reality and the other being in direct contact only with an inferior proposition. The difference is simply that the one is in a position to assert it as a truth and can substantiate his assertion: the other is not so placed; he is prepared to assert it, but does not claim that it is a truth and that he can substantiate it.

We can, I think, arrive at a simpler and more acceptable interpretation of the distinction between knowledge as objective and belief as subjective, if we remind ourselves of the connection between knowledge and learning. It is noticeable that those philosophers who are content to speak (metaphorically, we must suppose) of 'knowing reality' or of 'reality' as the object of knowledge fight shy of speaking of 'reality' as the object of learning, or of 'learning reality'. Whereas they may speak of 'learning facts', 'facts' cannot be regarded as 'entities' in the 'real world'. What we learn is, for example, that water is a combination of hydrogen and oxygen, that Paris is the capital of France, that lead is malleable, etc. Similarly, when we teach, in the sense of imparting knowledge, what we teach is that water is a combination of hydrogen and oxygen, etc. What we teach and what we learn are 'truths', not 'realities'. The need to express the distinction in mystifying ontological terms (the 'real' as opposed to the 'apparent' or 'reality' as opposed to 'pictures of reality') disappears if we abandon the general and abstract question, 'What is the object of knowledge?' and ask the more homely question, 'What sorts of things can I, or do I, learn, teach, know?'

The separate 'realms' of knowledge and belief are those of what is settled or established and what is still disputed. What we learn or teach or know is what is accepted as true: that lead is malleable, etc. What we believe, in the primary sense of belief, is what is not settled, what remains disputable. Thus, whereas one can know that Waterloo occurred in 1815, one cannot know that the Battle of Marathon was fought in 490 B.C. (I am assuming that the date is still in dispute). The proper 'attitude' in that connection is belief. Thus it is incongruous to say 'He knows that the Battle of Waterloo was fought in 1815, but I don't'. In this context (where something is settled) what goes for you must also go for me. I cannot concede your claim to be right without implying that I, too, would be right if I made the same claim. But, on the other hand, there is no inconsistency in my saying, 'He believes that brandy is good for heartburn, but I don't'. Here, where the issue is not settled, what goes for you need not also go for me. I am not committed to believing what you believe if I accept that you believe so-and-so. What is impossible is 'I believe that Marathon was fought in 490 B.C., but the Wykeham Professor knows it was in 491 B.C.'

The natural equation, then, is between 'what can be known' and 'what is settled' and between 'what can be believed' and 'what is not settled'. But there is a subsidiary sense of belief where we are sometimes prepared to say that someone believes what is settled. It is this lack of symmetry which, I think, has made plausible the identification of knowledge with true, justified belief. Thus, there may be situations where one might be prepared to say 'He believes that the Battle of Hastings was fought in 1066'. There is, however, an air of oddity about such a remark because of the fact that the normal expectation about generally accepted things is to say 'he knows'. Hence, to remove the oddity, it is necessary to qualify the expression by saying 'he *only* believes'. It would not, then, be in any way paradoxical to say, 'John knows that lead is malleable, but Bill only believes that it is'. What is being questioned in the refusing to use 'knows' of Bill is not that what he says is disputable or questionable, but rather his right to assert it as a truth. His reasons are deemed to be inadequate. In many circumstances, it might well be more apt to say 'Bill does not know' or 'Bill is just guessing' rather than 'Bill believes'. 'Believing' does not, of course, mean the same as 'guessing'.

We should, therefore, add a corrective to saying that what we know and what we believe is the same. What we know is what is, or can be, established, what is accepted as true: what we believe, in its primary sense, is what is not settled or what is still disputable. It is important to add the qualification 'what *can* be established', since we would not wish to rule out the possibility of saying of someone that he knew something when it had not been established or settled, or generally accepted as true: there have been solitary inventors who have discovered things which were not accepted until years afterwards. With this corrective in mind, we can understand the partiality for the 'fact' terminology, for saying that what we know are 'facts' and for refusing to say that what we believe are 'facts'. The expression 'what we know are "facts"', is unexceptionable, provided we do not regard facts as static chunks of reality which the knower 'inspects' or 'is confronted with', and which are beyond the sights or the reach of the believer. 'Facts' are what are generally accepted as true, for example that lead is malleable.

Thus the situations in which it is appropriate to use the expressions 'I know' and 'I believe' are different. Broadly speaking, the occasions where it is appropriate to say 'I believe' are those situations where the matter concerned has not been settled. We believe where it is not possible to know, where there is still room for doubt or dispute. Thus it would be quite appropriate for someone to say that he believed that the soul was immortal, whereas it would appear strange, at least to most of us, if someone said that he knew that the soul was immortal. If, *per impossibile*, it could be demonstrated that in fact the soul was immortal, the erstwhile believer would not then affirm that, in addition to believing it, he now knew that it was true. The appropriate thing for him to say would be, 'What I formerly believed, I now know to be true'.

But the appropriate use of 'I believe' is not only in those situations where we accept that, in principle, it is not possible for the issue to be settled. As Prichard remarked, belief is sometimes a stage in which we may be on the road to knowledge. I do not, of course, mean that belief is a mental state which we may pass through on the way to the state of knowledge. What is meant is that it is quite possible for an individual only to believe something the truth of which has been established. If he comes to know it, after inquiry or research perhaps, he no longer says that he believes, with all sorts of qualifications such as that his belief can be justified, that he is sure, etc. Very simply, he says 'I know'.

'Belief', then, is the appropriate term to use either (a) when knowledge just is not possible or (b) when the individual is not in a position to assert something categorically as a truth and can substantiate it. You can believe only where you do not know. This does *not* imply that where you know, you also have to believe.

A consequence of the distinction between knowledge as concerned with what is settled and belief as concerned with what is disputable is that there are connections between belief and such notions as 'debate', 'deliberation', 'alternatives', 'decision', etc. which are absent in the case of knowledge. Thus we argue or debate about our beliefs but not about what we know, since we can argue only about what is disputable. Beliefs can be 'controversial'; knowledge cannot be. Belief often follows deliberation; knowledge never does. Belief is appropriate where there are alternatives; we believe this-rather-than-that, but we do not say that we know this-rather-than-that. Adopting a belief is comparable with, or involves, making a decision; coming to know is not comparable with deciding. It makes sense to ask whether believing is voluntary or not, but it makes no sense to ask whether knowing is voluntary or not. 'Can I will to believe?' is a genuine philosophical conundrum: 'Can I will to know?' is not a question that concerns anyone. Dithering may prevent someone believing; it is not a hazard for knowers.

The distinction explains, further, why we sometimes speak of the boundaries or limits of knowledge, but not of the boundaries or limits of belief; only what is settled can have boundaries. But it must not, of course, be supposed that these boundaries are fixed and unalterable. What is not settled today may be settled tomorrow: it will then become 'knowledge', something which we can 'know' and teach as a 'fact'. But it also sometimes happens that what was accepted as knowledge yesterday is relegated today. Thus knowledge claims which may have been accepted at one time may later be rejected.

It is also consistent with the above distinction that there is quite a different relationship between knowledge and belief and the notion of commitment. The notion of commitment is relevant only where there is a risk that the person concerned may be mistaken. Thus we would not say that someone who knew that Great Britain is an island was committed to that item of knowledge. Conversely, we would be prepared to say of someone who believed something that he was committed to what he believed. The implicit suggestion is that he is prepared to act on something even though he does not know the answer. The reason is simply that there is no point in saying that someone is prepared to take a risk where an issue is already settled. In such a situation, nothing is at stake. We can also see why the notion of confidence is irrelevant to knowledge, why it cannot be a 'condition of knowledge'. Confidence is relevant where there is a risk, where the issue is not settled. A man is confident not about what he knows but about things where there is a risk of being wrong. The man who is confident of victory is the man who believes that he is going to win. Success dispenses with it. Confidence or the lack of it belongs to the world of the gambler; it is irrelevant where there is no risk of failure. If you believe that you are going to win the race, you can answer questions like 'How confident are you?' If you have won, the question is otiose. Confidence is relevant to learners; when you *have* learned something, the need for it has gone. Once I have learned that lead is malleable, how long do I have to stay confident of it? 'Convinced' means 'believes as firmly as possible, but cannot prove'.

The connection between knowledge and learning and the absence of a connection between believing and learning is instructive. Knowing is clearly intimately connected with learning. One comes to the position of knowing how to do something usually as the result of a process of learning, and similarly one comes to know that Paris is the capital of France as the result of learning it, which we may do in a variety of ways. But there is no such connection between learning and believing. 'How did you come to believe that brandy has beneficial properties?' cannot be answered by saying 'I learnt it in a medical text book'. Indeed, the very question 'How did you come to believe?' on the analogy of 'How did you come to know?' sounds inapt. Not only are the preliminaries to knowledge and belief different, their termination is also quite dissimilar. Thus, 'He no longer knows how to swim' or 'He no longer knows who the Presidents of the USA were', entail that he has forgotten what he once learnt. But 'He no longer believes that brandy has beneficial properties' does not mean that he has forgotten. It means that he has abandoned the belief, that he has changed his mind.

There is another aspect of the objective nature of knowledge and the subjective nature of belief which serves to differentiate the two. This is the sense in which one speaks of belief as a personal matter and of knowledge as a public matter. We think of what is known as public property, the sort of thing which is put in reference books or passed on from one generation to another. Knowledge tends to become anonymous whereas beliefs tend to be attributed to their owners. Thus encyclopaedias do not identify the knowers of the facts they list, but where they refer to what is still disputed, such as the date of the Battle of Marathon, they may well refer to persons or authorities, such as *The Cambridge Ancient History*, or 'Professor X believes it occurred in 491 B.C.' 'So-and-so believes . . .' occurs, but not 'so-and-so knows'. Thus, we contrast 'systems of belief' but not 'systems of knowledge'. We speak not of what the Russians know about politics, but what they believe: knowledge is international. Belief is 'personal' also in the sense that we speak of people cherishing their beliefs, being prepared to defend their beliefs, being reluctant to abandon them, etc. Beliefs may be eccentric or idiosyncratic: knowledge can be neither. Beliefs may be passionately held, but we tend to remain cool about what we know.

The differences between knowledge and belief which I have tried to illustrate all stem from the characteristic of 'knowing' which, following Professor Ryle, I described as an 'achievement' or 'success' verb. This, in my view, is the key both to the understanding of knowledge itself and to the difference between knowledge and belief. Whereas 'knowing' is a 'success' verb, 'believing' is not. Whereas 'knowing' necessarily implies that someone has got something right, 'believing' has no such implication. This explains why, in response to someone who says he knows something, i.e. is claiming a success, the question which we are apt to ask is 'How do you know?' The implication in the question is that the claimant should satisfy criteria which are commonly agreed. Before conceding knowledge claims we have to be satisfied not only that what is asserted to be true *is* true, but that the claimant has given, or can give, a proof or demonstration, etc. The determination that what is asserted *is* true is decided not by the individual's private criteria but by public criteria, and his justification is judged by public and not by private criteria. Criteria exist only for judging claims to be successful. We do not operate public criteria to assess whether a man believes something or not, except in the sense of assessing the reasonableness or sincerity of his belief. Whereas a failure to satisfy public criteria will disqualify a knowledge claim, failure to be able to show that one is right will not 'disallow' an affirmation of belief. It is in this vital sense that knowledge is 'objective' and belief 'subjective'.

Not all the advantages, however, fall on the side of knowledge. Things which are settled tend to become stale: issues which are still alive excite and retain our interest. Except in special circumstances, such as quizzes and examinations, we are more interested in a man's beliefs than in his knowledge. Genuine researchers lose interest in their hypotheses when they are established: they move on to new explorations. The heat and the excitement are over.

We should be on our guard against the simple identification of intelligence with knowledge, either in the sense of learning what is already known or accepted, or in the sense of knowing how to do something which we have been taught, for example knowing how to cook an omelette. Intelligence is displayed not so much in assimilating other people's discoveries but in the way in which we tackle issues which are still uncertain or undecided. Fertility in constructing hypotheses, which comes under the heading of belief rather than knowledge, is the mark of intelligence and not the ability to repeat what others have discovered. Belief and knowledge are not, of course, in any sort of opposition: the ability to construct hypotheses needs a spring-board of knowledge, and hypotheses are constructed in the hope that they will become established. They are fellow workers in the same field, not rivals.

In view of the differences which exist between knowledge and belief, it is not surprising that attempts to define knowledge in terms of belief have failed to gain general acceptance. Plato in the *Theaetetus* showed, I think, the right instinct in having nothing to do with such attempts, though we may not perhaps accept the reasons which he gives for refusing to accept the identification of knowledge with 'true opinion' or 'true belief'. The difficulty in distinguishing between knowledge and belief has been accentuated by Platonic and post-Platonic attempts to locate them in different and separate 'worlds', as if 'objective' meant 'having reality as its object' and 'subjective' meant 'having pictures of reality' as its object. Equally harmful have been attempts to identify some unique psychological criterion for distinguishing between two antipathetic 'states of mind'. But if we succeed in divesting knowledge of irrelevant accretions such as notions of 'infallibility', either in terms of 'being concerned with reality', or in terms of 'unique, incorrigible experiences', and concentrate on the implications of 'knowing' as an 'achievement' or 'success' word, the difference between knowledge and belief is easier to draw. But knowledge will not then appear to be quite the mysterious, nor perhaps the exciting, thing which we have for so long supposed it to be.

Bibliographical Notes

In this essay I have not attempted to review the literature on the topics discussed. For those readers who wish to pursue these topics further, I append a representative list of works for their consideration.

A. Books on the Theory of Knowledge

1. Aaron, R. I., *Knowing and the Function of Reason* (Oxford: The Clarendon Press, 1971).
2. Ackermann, R. J., *Belief and Knowledge* (London: Macmillan, 1972).
3. Armstrong, D. M., *Belief, Truth and Knowledge* (Cambridge University Press, 1973).
4. Austin, J. L., *Sense and Sensibilia* (Oxford: The Clarendon Press, 1962).
5. Ayer, A. J., *The Foundations of Empirical Knowledge* (London: Macmillan, 1940).
6. Ayer, A. J., *The Problem of Knowledge* (Penguin Books, 1956).
7. Chisholm, R. M., *Perceiving: A Philosophical Study* (Ithaca, N.Y.: Cornell University Press, 1957).
8. Chisholm, R. M., *Theory of Knowledge* (Englewood Cliffs, N.J.: Prentice-Hall, 1966).
9. Ginet, C., *Knowledge, Perception, and Memory* (Dordrecht: D. Reidel, 1975).
10. Hamlyn, D. W., *The Theory of Knowledge* (London: Macmillan, 1970).
11. Hintikka, Jaakko, *Knowledge and Belief* (Ithaca, N.Y.: Cornell University Press, 1962).
12. Hintikka, Jaakko, *Knowledge and the Known* (Dordrecht: D. Reidel, 1974).
13. Lehrer, K., *Knowledge* (Oxford: The Clarendon Press, 1974).
14. Pears, David, *What is Knowledge?* (London: Allen & Unwin, 1972).
15. Quinton, A., *The Nature of Things* (London and Boston: Routledge & Kegan Paul, 1973) especially Part II.
16. Ryle, G., *The Concept of Mind* (London: Hutchinson, 1949).
17. Vendler, Z., *Res Cogitans* (Cornell University Press, 1972).
18. Wittgenstein, L., *On Certainty* (Oxford: Blackwell, 1969).
19. Woozley, A. D., *Theory of Knowledge* (London: Hutchinson, 1949).

B. Articles

1. Austin, J. L., 'Other Minds', *Proceedings of the Aristotelian Society*, Supplementary Volume XX (1946); reprinted in Austin, J. L., *Philosophical Papers*, 2nd ed. (Oxford University Press, 1970).
2. Geach, P. T., 'Assertion', *Philosophical Review*, Vol. LXXIV (1965) 449–465.
3. Gettier, Edmund L., 'Is Justified True Belief Knowledge?', *Analysis*, Vol. 23 (1963) 121–3.
4. Harrison, J., 'Knowing and Promising', *Mind*, Vol. 71 (1962) 443–57.
5. Harrison, J., 'Does Knowing imply Believing?', *Philosophical Quarterly*, Vol. 13 (1963) 322–32.
6. Malcolm, N., 'Knowledge and Belief', *Mind*, Vol. 51 (1952) 178–89.
7. Price, H. H., 'Some Considerations about Belief', *Proceedings of the Aristotelian Society*, Vol. 35 (1934–5) 229–52.
8. Radford, C., 'Knowledge-By Examples', *Analysis*, Vol. 27 (1966) 1–11.
9. Radford, C., '"Analysing" 'Know(s) That'', *Philosophical Quarterly*, Vol. 20 (1970) 222–9.
10. Ryle, G., 'Knowing How and Knowing That', *Proceedings of the Aristotelian Society*, Vol. 46 (1945–6) 1–16.
11. Urmson, J. O., 'Parenthetical Verbs', *Mind*, Vol. 61 (1952) 480–96.
12. White, Alan R., 'On claiming to Know', *Philosophical Review*, Vol. 66 (1957) 180–92.
13. Woozley, A. D., 'Knowing and Not Knowing', *Proceedings of the Aristotelian Society*, Vol. 53 (1952–3) 151–72.

Nos. 3, 4, 6, 7, 12, 13, are reprinted in A. Phillips Griffiths (ed.), *Knowledge and Belief* (Oxford University Press, 1967). This book contains a very full bibliography and an excellent introduction. On the topic of perception, readers should consult the articles reprinted in G. J. Warnock (ed.), *The Philosophy of Perception* (Oxford University Press, 1967) and the bibliography.

Index